Gracious Insights

Gracious Insights

By Katina Moore

Tampa, Florida

Gracious Insights

Library of Congress Control Number: 2022950200

ISBN (paperback): 9781662934780
eISBN: 9781662934797

Published by Gatekeeper Press
7853 Gunn Hwy, Suite 209
Tampa, FL 33626
www.GatekeeperPress.com

This book is dedicated to the ones in my life that have kept the faith, and finished their course; my dad, my step mom, and my step dad. Everything that I have learned from each of their walks with the Lord has been a great blessing to me.

Leavy Cooper
August 4, 1944 - April 16, 2019

Carolyn Cooper
May 13, 1955 - July 8, 2019

Dennis Coatney
March 5, 1962 - September 10, 2021

Acknowledgments

There are a multitude of people who I owe thanks to for the contents of this book. They are all people that I have had the privilege of meeting throughout my life. The people that I had the occasion to sit in church with, as well as those who have ministered alongside me, and to me, in one form or another. Most all of these have taken opportunity, at one time or another, to speak truth into my life, thereby enabling me to grow in my own walk and relationship with the Lord.

Being raised in church, I have had the opportunity to go to a number of churches of differing denominations. I can say now that not one of them do I consider a mistake, or a detour that I shouldn't have taken in my life's journey. I have gained knowledge from each one of them that has enabled me to grow spiritually. I thank each and every one of the ministers that I have had the privilege of hearing.

I want to thank Jesus Christ for everything I have experienced, and everything I know of Him up to this point in my life. It is my sincere prayer that I learn even more.

I thank my Mom, Cynthia Coatney, for listening to me read and go on and on about this book before it was finished. She always has been and continues to be my earthly stability. I love you, Mama.

I thank my niece, Chandra Griffin, for all of her hard work on this project. Without her assistance and encouragement, I may not have finished it at all. I love you, Chan. Thank you for believing in me.

Foreword

I am so thankful and humbled by all that the Lord has shown me. I love the Lord and I love His Word. I enjoy studying and learning all that I can pertaining to Him. The Lord has given me what I like to call "gracious insights" during the course of my studies. Sometimes it starts with a single word that He prompts me to study. Sometimes it will be by something I have read. He also speaks to me through things that I experience from day to day.

I have shared many of these thoughts and studies with people around me. And although I usually write them down, I never imagined putting all of them together as a book. But, as I was pondering this thought, the Lord brought to me a couple of different verses...

Colossians 4:16 says, "And when this epistle is read among you, cause that it be read also in the church of the Laodiceans; and that ye likewise read the epistle from Laodicea."

1 Thessalonians 5:27 says, "I charge you by the Lord that this epistle be read unto all the holy brethren."

I believe this means that we are to share revelations we receive from the Lord. I believe that it gives hope and encouragement to others as we do. I know that I love to hear or read of things that the Lord has shown to someone else. It is my hope and prayer that you are blessed and encouraged by some, if not all, of the insights that the Lord has so graciously shown to me.

Sincerely,
Katina Moore

Table of Contents

A Letter from the Lord

Philemon 1:1-7 says, "Paul, a prisoner of Jesus Christ, and Timothy our brother, unto Philemon our dearly beloved, and fellowlabourer, And to our beloved Apphis, and Archippus our fellowsoldier, and to the church in thy house: Grace to you, and peace, from God our Father and the Lord Jesus Christ. I thank my God, making mention of thee always in my prayers, Hearing of thy love and faith, which thou hast toward the Lord Jesus, and toward all saints; That the communication of thy faith may become effectual by the acknowledging of every good thing which is in you in Christ Jesus. For we have great joy and consolation in thy love, because the bowels of the saints are refreshed by thee, brother."

-This epistle, or letter, begins by letting the reader know that; it is from Paul, and that it is primarily written to Philemon.

-Paul then lets Philemon know that he and Timothy have heard of the love and faith Philemon has toward Jesus and all saints, and that he is refreshing to the saints.

VS 8) "Wherefore, though I might be much bold in Christ to enjoin thee that which is convenient,"

VS 9) "Yet for love's sake I rather beseech thee, being such an one as Paul the aged, and now also a prisoner of Jesus Christ."

-In verses 8 and 9, Paul is saying that although he COULD enjoin (INSTRUCT) Philemon, he would rather (for love's sake) beseech (ASK or BEG) him

-Paul is about to ASK Philemon to do something that he could TELL him to do.

Verses 10-14…"I beseech thee for my son Onesimus, whom I have begotten in my bonds: Which in time past was to thee unprofitable, but now profitable to thee and to me: Whom I have sent again: thou therefore receive him, that is, mine own bowels: Whom I would have retained with me, that in thy stead he might have ministered unto me in the bonds of the gospel: But without thy mind would I do nothing; that thy benefit should not be as it were of necessity, but willingly."

-Philemon was the host of a house church in Colosse. Onesimus had been Philemon's slave, but had stolen from Philemon and run away to Rome. That made Onesimus a runaway slave and a thief.

-Onesimus came into contact with Paul, who was imprisoned in Rome, and was converted to Christianity.

-Paul is sending Onesimus back to Philemon because he technically belongs to Philemon, AND has stolen from him.

Verses 15-17…"For perhaps he therefore departed for a season, that thou shouldest receive him for ever; Not now as a servant, but above a servant, a brother beloved, specially to me, but how much more unto thee, both in the flesh, and in the Lord? If thou count me therefore a partner, receive him as myself."

-So, Paul is "asking" Philemon not only to receive Onesimus as if he were Paul himself, but also to free him from his status as Philemon's slave.

Verses 18-19…"If he hath wronged thee, or oweth thee ought, put that on mine account; I Paul have written it with mine own hand, I will repay it: albeit I do not say to thee how thou owest unto me even thine own self besides."

-Now, Paul is "asking" Philemon to cancel the debt Onesimus owes, saying that he (Paul) will pay the debt for Onesimus if Philemon still requires it, IN SPITE OF the fact that Philemon owes Paul himself.

Verses 20-21..."Yea, brother, let me have joy of thee in the Lord: refresh my bowels in the Lord. Having confidence in thy obedience I wrote unto thee, knowing that thou wilt also do more than I say."

-Here, Paul lets Philemon know that he expects Philemon not only to grant his "request", but to go even beyond that in welcoming Onesimus.

As I was studying this one-chapter book, I was reminded of another passage of Scripture...

2 Timothy 3:16-17 says, "All scripture is given by inspiration of God, and is profitable for doctrine, for reproof, for correction, for instruction in righteousness: That the man of God may be perfect, throughly furnished unto all good works."

I know it says ALL SCRIPTURE. But, I had to ask the Lord why this brief letter to Philemon about Onesimus was relevant to the church of today. AND WOW!!!

ARE YOU READY FOR THIS?!? THIS IS FOR ALL OF US!!!

I'M GOING TO WRITE A LETTER TO THE CHURCH "FROM THE LORD"!!! ABOUT RUNAWAYS!!!

My Beloved, I have seen your love and faith toward Myself, as well as, to all saints. I have great joy and consolation in thy love, because the bowels of the saints are refreshed by thee. And although I could command you, I would rather make a request, thereby giving you the opportunity to do this willingly. I AM sending someone back to you that I consider to be My son. I realize that he has done things in the past that may cause you to have hard feelings toward him. You may even feel that he owes you. But, I AM asking you to receive him as My Own Self. And if you still feel that he owes you anything, in spite of the fact that you owe Me, put it on My account. I will pay his debt Myself. It will be Joy to Me, because I have confidence in your obedience, knowing that you will do even more than I ask. Sincerely, Jesus

OH MY! OH MY! OH MY!

How many times does someone "backslide" or "leave" the church, only to never want to return because of how they will be "received"? Or NOT RECEIVED?

If the Lord draws or sends them back, WHO ARE WE to make them feel that they owe us A THING? HOW CAN WE THINK THAT THEY HAVE TO PROVE THEMSELVES TO US? LET ALONE, TELL THEM THAT THEY HAVE TO PROVE THEMSELVES TO US! This tells me that we (THE CHURCH) are supposed to receive them as the Lord Himself! That if we think they owe us anything, HE WILL PAY IT! We should be thinking of what WE OWE THE LORD!

And one more thing; if we do feel that they owe us anything, since the Lord said He would pay it, ARE WE GONNA GO ASK HIM FOR IT??? OH, WE BETTER NOT!

After His Heart

This is Samuel talking to King Saul.

1 Samuel 13:14 says, "But now thy kingdom shall not continue: the Lord hath sought him a man after his own heart, and the Lord hath commanded him to be captain over his people, because thou hast not kept that which the Lord commanded thee."

Acts 13:22 says, "And when he had removed him, he raised up unto them David to be their king; to whom also he gave testimony, and said, I have found David the son of Jesse, a man after mine own heart, which shall fulfil all my will."

As I read these passages, I wondered why David was "after God's own heart" if God already loves us.

And He does.

I have heard the phrase "a woman after my own heart". It is referring to a woman who has cooked a delicious meal for a man. If the man really enjoys the meal, he says that she's a woman after his own heart. Right?

I've also heard the phrase "the way to a man's heart is through his stomach". The delicious meal, right?

She wants to impress him. She wants to please him. She wants him to approve of her, her efforts, her cooking skills. She wants him to like her, to love her. Right?

Well, God ALREADY loved David. So, why was David after God's heart?

Yes, David wanted to please God.

BUT...

David wanted God's heart! He wanted to LOVE like God loves, to show MERCY and COMPASSION like God does, to FORGIVE like God forgives. He wanted to see through God's eyes, with justice, love, and grace.

David wasn't after trying to get God to love him. HE ALREADY DID.

Lord, help me today to be a woman after your heart. To love and forgive with all that I am. To show mercy and compassion and to extend grace as freely as You do. Enable me to see through Your eyes.

Lord, show me the way to have Your heart, in Jesus' Name.

Be Obedient

Several years ago, my sister had left home here in Florida to go to North Dakota. She was by herself and had gone by bus. While on the bus, she met a lady who had a little boy. The little boy was crying because he was hungry.

My sister went with the lady and the little boy to buy him some food. Somewhere along the way my sister's wallet was stolen. If it was the lady or someone else, I don't know.

But when the bus got to the station in Chicago, my sister didn't have her wallet. She had no money. She had nothing except the ticket that had already been paid for to North Dakota. She was crying. She was sick. She didn't know what to do.

So, she called home and told us the situation she was in. She was sitting against the wall in the bus station in Chicago.

Again, she was sick, alone, no money, no food, no identification, and very upset.

We started praying.

I told the Lord that I know He has children all over this earth. I told Him that He knew I had no way to get to my sister. I told him that I needed Him to send one of His children to her to help her.

A little while later, she called again. A security guard had come to her. PRAISE JESUS! He not only gave her some food vouchers, but he bought her medicine too. PRAISE JESUS!

You have come too late to tell me that God won't do it!

Now, I know the Lord had to speak to that man to go help my sister. I am so very thankful that He did. I am also very thankful that the man was willing and obedient.

So, you never know when you hear that still small voice or you feel that gentle urging, what the Lord may want you to do. You don't know if there is someone who is sick, alone, no food, no money, someone's loved one. So be obedient.

Lord, I thank You for hearing and answering our prayers that day. I also thank You that the man at the bus station was willing and obedient. I ask that You continue to bless him for his obedience. I ask that You enable me to hear and to know when You want me to go and help someone. Help me to be obedient when

You would tell me to go, in Jesus' Name.

Be Victorious

You can be a strong, "manly" man, carry, and OWN the fear of those around you (in the natural), and still be as weak as a kitten spiritually. You can come out of each and every battle "victorious" (in the natural), but as soon as a spiritual attack is launched against you, not only do you not see it coming, often you fall flat on your face.

Take a look at Samson. His story can be found in the book of Judges, chapters 13-16. His strength was unequaled. Yet, when the attack was launched at him through Delilah, he fell. Do you think Samson would have handed Delilah the secret to his strength if he had been spiritually stronger so that he might have seen the attack for what it was?

Again, you can be a man of God, spiritually strong, have a wealth of knowledge, and still fall flat on your face during a spiritual attack. Take a look at Moses. His story can be found in the book of Numbers, chapter 20. Moses walked so closely with God that he led God's chosen people and received the Ten

Commandments, as well as the "blueprints" for the first tabernacle. Yet, when he experienced frustration with the people, when discipline was required, Moses fell. This one act of "lashing out" in frustration cost him the promised land.

Moses had worked for and walked toward something for many, many years. But in the end, he was only able to view it from a distance. Do you think Moses would have reacted differently if he had seen the attack for what it was?

Romans 12:3 says, "For I say, through the grace given unto me, to every man that is among you, not to think of himself more highly than he ought to think; but to think soberly, according as God hath dealt to every man the measure of faith."

No matter how strong or knowledgeable we are in the natural, and no matter how close to God we are, we are still susceptible to the onslaught of the enemy's warfare. We cannot assume that we will make it through just because of "who we are". Also, we never know how long-lasting or how intense an attack will be. We MUST keep our eyes open so that we may not only see his attacks for what they are, but also that we will be able to overcome his plots and schemes. This is the ONLY way we will come through each battle VICTORIOUS!

Body Parts

Have you ever had an ear ache, a sprain or broken bone, a torn ligament, a pulled muscle, a stubbed toe, an ingrown toenail, a "hammered" finger, a splinter, a burn or blister, a mouth ulcer? How about something more serious? Like loss of hearing, loss of vision, cancer, liver problems, kidney problems, heart problems, arthritis, pneumonia, a tumor, a slipped disk?

What did you do about it? Did you curse it, cast it off or out, declare it forever useless? Did you cut it off?

Did you decide it was no longer any good? Or that it couldn't be helped?

Or did you pray for it, go up for prayer in a church service, or call people to pray? Did you call the doctor? Or go to the emergency room? Did you take medicine? Did you do everything in your power to get it fixed or healed to make the pain or sickness go away so that you could use the part again?

There is a specific reason or use for each and every body part that we have. Each part has to be fully functional: each has to be present, not in pain, not sick, to be able to perform its duty. If we have no eyes, we can't see. If we have no feet, we can't walk. If we have no legs, we can't stand. If we have no hands, there are a multitude of things that we can't do. If we have no tongue, we can't speak. If we have no ears, we can't hear. I could go on and on, because there are so many different parts in our bodies, and they are there for a reason. They are required for our bodies to function the way God created them to function.

Our individual human bodies are made up of many parts, and each has its own assigned task. By now, you probably know where this is going. Our bodies are a very small replica of the Body of Christ, which is the Church. It is one body, but it is made up of many parts that each have an assigned task.

1 Corinthians 12:12 says, "For as the body is one, and hath many members, and all the members of that one body, being many, are one body: so also is Christ."

Verse 14 says, "For the body is not one member, but many."

Verses 25-26 say, "That there should be no schism (or divide) in the body; but that the members should have the same care one for another. And whether one member suffer, all the members suffer with it; or one member be honored, all the members rejoice with it."

We need to treat this body, the Body of Christ, the Church, and its parts with as much care and importance as we do our own individual bodies. If we know that a part (member) is in pain or sick, we need to do all that we can to help them to be healed and become fully functional again.

Bring It!

It doesn't matter who we are, or what our gifts and callings are, sometimes we feel that our efforts and offerings are inadequate. It seems that everyone else "brings so much more to the table" than we do.

Luke 21:1-3 says, "And he looked up, and saw the rich men casting their gifts into the treasury. And he saw also a certain poor widow casting in thither two mites. And he said, Of a truth I say unto you, that this poor widow hath cast in more than they all:"

For example: If we are to have a banquet...and you imagine that everyone else will bring an array of the finest foods, cooked to perfection, in the most beautifully matching dishes...you are excited about the banquet, and you look in your cupboard to see what you may bring...all you have is a pack of plastic forks...so now you are not so excited...you may not even go...it would be embarrassing to just bring a pack of plastic forks when everyone else is bringing ALL those other wonderful things...then you hear a still small voice encouraging you to go and to bring the forks...when you get to the banquet, you find that you were right, everyone else brought all that beautiful, awesome-smelling food...BUT no one brought forks...now you are glad you brought the forks, for without them, no one would be able to eat...

No matter how small our gifts and offerings may seem, they are needed, they are wanted, they are beneficial, they are essential...TO ALL...DO NOT let the enemy tell you that you have nothing to offer... because you do.

Called and Chosen

During prayer, I have been thanking the Lord for "calling and choosing" me. I have also been thanking Him for placing me where He has placed me in church, while at the same time asking Him to help me to be ALL that He created and has called and chosen me to be, as well as to enable me to do ALL that He would have me to do.

A few days ago, this is what He said to me…"You are not completely ready. I AM still working on you.

You know that I have made some changes in the way you think, feel, act, react, and respond. But I AM perfecting My work in you. Seek Me in EVERYTHING, FOR EVERYONE, FOR YOURSELF. I want you to appreciate and be TRULY THANKFUL."

Matthew 22:14 says, "For many are called, but few are chosen."

First, let me tell you that WE ARE NOT just CALLED! WE ARE CHOSEN! To be CHOSEN is a higher CALLING than to just be CALLED! To be CHOSEN not only carries a higher level of BLESSINGS, but also a higher level of RESPONSIBILITY and SELF-DISCIPLINE! He wants His work PERFECTED in us, the CALLED AND CHOSEN!! OH, MY GOODNESS!!

TODAY, we HAVE TO know, WE ARE NOT just going different places and moving around at random!

WE ARE BEING PLACED!! WE ARE NOT the ones opening the doors that NO MAN CAN CLOSE!!

HE IS!! OH, MY MY!!

God is getting ready to do something SPECTACULAR!! He is GETTING US READY to BE A PART OF IT!! PRAISE THE LORD!!

We say that we "ain't seen nothing yet" and we say we have only just "scratched the surface". BUT DO WE BELIEVE IT?? OH, MY WE BETTER BELIEVE IT!! He's about to show us something like we've NEVER SEEN!!

Isaiah 43:18-19 says, "Remember ye not the former things, neither consider the things of old. Behold, I WILL DO A NEW THING; NOW IT SHALL SPRING FORTH; SHALL YE NOT KNOW IT? I will even make a way in the wilderness, and rivers in the desert"... OH LORD!! We won't even remember or consider what is PAST!! He's about to do something that is BEYOND AMAZING!! OH, LET'S GET READY, STAY READY, AND BE READY!!

Oh, thank you, Lord, that I get to be a part of Your plan! Thank you, Lord that You have a place just for me! Thank you, Lord that You haven't given up on me, but You are perfecting Your work in me! Thank You for calling and choosing me and enabling me to be all that You created me to be! Lord, I know that I know that I know that I could never be anything without Your help!

Lord, I ask not only for myself, but for ALL of us, that You will enable us to be EVERYTHING that You have CALLED and CHOSEN us to be. Help us, O Lord, to know that we know that we know WHAT WE NEED TO BE DOING and that we are DOING it, in Jesus' Name.

Come Back

As I lay in bed praying, I was just asking the Lord where my useful place is. What can I do?

What can I say? And aside from praying, how can I help? Specific Scriptures began to come to my mind, and with them a message for a specific people, that was very clear.

I only claim to be a vessel that is willing to be used of the Lord, and I am very thankful for that. I want to be obedient to the Lord.

2 Chronicles 7:14 says, "If my people, which are called by my name, shall humble themselves, and pray, and seek my face, and turn from their wicked ways; then will I hear from heaven, and will forgive their sin, and will heal their land."

These are people who have been called by the Lord, but have since gone down a different road that took them away from Him.

"Backsliders", they are called.

Jeremiah 3:14 says, "O backsliding children, saith the Lord; for I am married unto you:"

Romans 11:29 says, "For the gifts and calling of God are without repentance." (That means they don't go away!)

It doesn't matter how far you have gone down that "wrong" road. If you have built a new house or life there, if the "vehicle" that took you there is broken down, it is NOT too late to start heading back!

Please come back! The Lord is married to you and HE IS FAITHFUL! He is holding the door open, waiting for you!

If your faith is weak or maybe you feel you have simply gone too far, if you are reading this,

YOU HAVE NOT!

Romans 10:17 says, "So then faith cometh by hearing, and hearing by the word of God."

Before you give up, or throw in the towel, or quit trying, give Him a chance to increase your faith by hearing the Word of God. Give Him a chance to show you.

Hebrews 10:25 says, "Not forsaking the assembling of ourselves together, as the manner of some is, but EXHORTING ONE ANOTHER: and so much the more, as ye see the day approaching."

We have gone through a time of being separated this year so that some of us may not have been able to assemble together. But, the middle of that verse says "EXHORTING ONE ANOTHER",

I can do that!

To exhort means to strongly encourage or to urge someone to do something, to beg, to plead.

I am here to exhort you, to strongly encourage and urge you, to beg and to plead with you. Turn back to God. He still loves you and I do too. He is our ONLY hope. No matter what lies the enemy tries to tell you, the Lord loves you and He is waiting with open door and open arms for you to come back! I pray that you are encouraged and I pray that you turn and reach toward Him today, in Jesus' Name.

Comfort Zone to Promised Land

First of all, God chose the children of Israel unto Himself...and WE are chosen today!

Exodus 3: 7,8 says, "And the Lord said, I have surely seen the affliction of my people which are in Egypt, and have heard their cry by reason of their taskmasters; for I know their sorrows; And I am come down to deliver them out of the hand of the Egyptians, and to bring them up out of that land unto a good land and a large, unto a land flowing with milk and honey;"

This is the promise God made to bring the people out.

Exodus 16:3 says, "And the children of Israel said unto them, Would to God we had died by the hand of the Lord in the land of Egypt, when we sat by the flesh pots, and when we did eat bread to the full; for ye have brought us forth into this wilderness, to kill this whole assembly with hunger."

This is the people complaining because God brought them out--OF THEIR COMFORT ZONE!

Egypt obviously wasn't a perfect place for them if they were "afflicted" and had "sorrows" and God heard their "cry"...but apparently, they were comfortable there...more comfortable anyway than they were when taking the steps required to go unto the land God had promised them. Deuteronomy 11:10-12 says, "For the land, whither thou goest thou goest in to possess it, is not as the land of Egypt, from whence ye came out, where thou sowedst thy seed, and wateredst it with thy foot, as a garden of herbs: But the land, whither ye go to possess it, is a land of hills and valleys, and drinketh water of the rain of heaven: A land which the Lord thy God careth for: the eyes of the Lord thy God are always upon it, from the beginning of the year even unto the end of the year."

God was trying to get them to accept the promise He made them. He wasn't advertising or trying to play it up. He was simply trying to let them know that what He had promised them was so much better than what they were used to or comfortable with.

Joshua 21:43-45 says, "And the Lord gave unto Israel all the land which he sware to give unto their fathers; and they possessed it, and dwelt therein. And the Lord gave them rest round about, according to all that he sware unto their fathers: and there stood not a man of all their enemies before them; the Lord delivered all their enemies into their hand. There failed not aught of any good thing which the Lord had spoken unto the house of Israel; all came to pass."

WOW!!! Now if that don't make you want to step out of that comfort zone and head toward your

Promised Land!!! Lord, help and enable us today to leave the places in which we have made ourselves comfortable to the point that the journey toward our promised land seems more daunting than staying. Grant us the wisdom and the strength that is required to take the first step, to make the journey, and to possess what You have promised us, in Jesus' Name.

Commitment

First, I know I've said before that I was raised in church. BUT, I never really had a RELATIONSHIP with the Lord when I was growing up. Oh, I went to the altar, when He would speak something through someone that touched my heart or made me feel conviction. At the time, I don't think I even knew what to call conviction. As I grew older, I walked on paths that I chose for myself, just doing what I wanted to do.

He protected me, THANK YOU, LORD, even though I was "running" from Him. I don't think I knew what to call that either. But that's what it was.

Then, when He helped me to FINALLY figure out that I wasn't the one who knew what was best for me, He called me back. I repented, again, and I think I was excited about "trying" to "live right". But actually committing to TRY to live right took some time. And when I had only gone so far as to commit to TRY, I thought I had accomplished something huge. BUT, He had a different approach in mind for me. He wanted me FULLY COMMITTED to Him. When I first knew this, I hesitated. I thought, "I know I will just mess up again." It seriously took SEVERAL WEEKS of me mentally arguing with Him. I would say,

"I just don't think I will be able to do it." Then He would just gently pull at me again and say,

"With My help, you can."

I don't think I could ever explain to you what a RELIEF it was when He finally convinced me to COMMIT to living for Him to the best of my effort and ability. I guess I didn't realize what just the back and forth struggle in my mind was doing to my peace of mind. That was several years ago. And I have been far from perfect during that time. I have failed. I have struggled. I have stumbled and fell flat on my face. I have had to repent again and again. I still have to repent. I am still learning. I have overcome some things. Some things I still battle. BUT, THANK GOD FOR URGING ME TO MAKE THAT COMMITMENT!! AND THANK GOD FOR HELPNG ME TO MEAN IT WHEN I MADE IT!! AND OH MY!! I THANK HIM FOR LETTING ME KNOW THAT HE WOULD HELP ME AND WITH HIS HELP I CAN MAKE IT!!

I said all of that to say this; if you are in the midst of the SEVERAL WEEKS that I mentioned, where you are wanting to try living for the Lord, but you're just not sure if you can do it without failure, I would like to join the Lord in urging you to FULLY COMMIT to live for Him to the best of your effort and ability.

You have to know, going in, that you will fail, you will stumble, and you will fall, BUT the Word says in Psalm 37:23-24, "The steps of a good man are ordered by the Lord: and he delighteth in his way. Though he fall, HE SHALL NOT BE UTTERLY CAST DOWN: FOR THE LORD UPHOLDETH HIM WITH HIS HAND." Like I said, I am still learning. I do not profess to "know it all", but this I do know... He will help, He does help, NONE of us can do it without His help.

So, I urge you today, to make that commitment. GET ALL IN and GO ALL OUT for Him! He is waiting for you. He has something for you to do that ONLY you can do. It is not only for your benefit, but for the benefit of the ENTIRE BODY OF CHRIST! THE WHOLE WORLD!!

Confidence

James 5:16 says, "Confess your faults one to another, and pray one for another, that ye may be healed. The effectual fervent prayer of a righteous man availeth much."

If you have a problem or you are in the midst of a battle, you should be able to confide in a brother or sister. And being that brother or sister, you should be able to keep that confidence. We are instructed in the Word to tell one another, so that we can pray for one another. This is NOT intended to be fuel for the "grapevine".

I have experienced faults and failures during the course of my walk. Who hasn't?

I have confessed those faults to a Godly friend who, instead of praying for me, betrayed that confidence.

Why? Only they and the Lord know. Maybe to hide a fault of their own. Maybe to make themselves seem more spiritual than me. I don't know.

But, I have also confessed faults to a Godly friend who kept that confidence. And not only that, they took it to the Lord in earnest prayer. They didn't judge me. They prayed for me. They told the ONLY One who could help. And He already knew about it. Can you see the difference in these two situations? The first one caused me more sorrow than I had in the beginning. It also cost me what I had considered to be a Godly friend. The second one not only helped me through a tough battle of temptation, it caused me to have faith in the fact that some people are actually willing to help in the way that we are instructed in the Word. By

only taking your confidence to the Lord in prayer.

Discretion means, the quality of behaving or speaking in such a way as to avoid causing offense or revealing private information.

If you have faults, confess them to a Godly person who has discretion. Someone who will ONLY take it to the Lord. Someone who will pray for you as if they are the one in the midst of the battle. Lord, I thank You for Godly friends. I thank You for Godly friends with discretion. If someone confesses a fault to me, I ask that You help me to always be a trustworthy friend who will earnestly pray for them, without betraying their confidence to others, in Jesus' Name.

Conviction and Condemnation

Conviction

To convict means to prove or to find (a person) guilty.

John 8:9 says, "And they which heard it, being convicted by their own conscience, went out one by one, beginning at the eldest, even unto the last: and Jesus was left alone, and the woman standing in the midst."

This passage of Scripture is referring to the woman who was "taken" in the very act of adultery. The Pharisees took her to Jesus saying that the law stated that she should be stoned. These men proved and found her guilty. Jesus, on the other hand, more or less let them know that they had placed themselves in a seat that wasn't theirs, the judge's seat, to convict her. He said, "He that is without sin among you, let him first cast a stone at her."

John 16:7-8 says, "Nevertheless I tell you the truth; It is expedient for you that I go away: for if I go not away, the Comforter will not come unto you; but if I depart, I will send him unto you.

And when he is come, he will reprove (convict) the world of sin, and of righteousness, and of judgment."

To convict here means to cause to see; or to illuminate.

This passage of Scripture tells us who is to convict. It is not us. It is the Holy Spirit. He convicts us, or causes us to see where we take a wrong turn on our journey. He causes us to feel this conviction within our own conscience. This conviction should not be coming from a fellow believer. It is not our job to convict one another.

Condemnation

Condemn means to disapprove of strongly, to declare guilty, to pass sentence on, to judge, to decide or to declare unfit for use.

Luke 6:37 says, "Judge not, and ye shall not be judged: condemn not, and ye shall not be condemned: forgive, and ye shall be forgiven:"

Romans 8:34 says, "Who is he that condemneth? It is Christ that died, yea rather, that is risen again, who is even at the right hand of God, who also maketh intercession for us."

Romans 15:7 says, "Wherefore receive ye one another, as Christ also received us to the glory of God."

Again, condemnation is something that is NOT our job.

Ask yourself these questions...

Have I ever tried to prove someone guilty of "sin" to someone else or just felt it in my heart about someone? Have I ever, within my own self, just strongly disapproved of someone? Have I ever declared someone guilty, passed sentence on them, or judged them about something, in my own mind? Have I ever decided that the Lord shouldn't be using someone due to "sin" that I felt they had committed, and declared in my own mind that they were unfit for use?

Did I pray for them? Do I realize that the judge's seat is somewhere I do not belong? Will I pray for myself?

Lord, I thank You for the Holy Spirit. Help us to remember that we are not to judge one another, convict, or condemn one another. Help us to encourage and lift each other up. Enable us to receive one another while allowing the Holy Spirit to do what You sent Him to do, in Jesus' Name.

Conviction to Conversion?

To convict means to convince or reprove of sin or wrongdoing. It's that lesson or message or even just a spoken word that you hear that lets you know you are doing or have been doing something wrong, and you need to change.

John 16:8 says, "And when he (the Holy Spirit) is come, he will REPROVE the world of sin, and of righteousness, and of judgment:"

"While the Spirit persuades human beings of guilt and convinces them of judgment to come, conviction alone does not produce conversion."- The Revell Concise Bible Dictionary

The word conviction is originally derived from two Latin terms meaning "cause to see"...conversion means to change. So, the Holy Spirit "causes us to see" that we need to change,

BUT conversion is our choice. We have to CHOOSE to change.

During Peter's sermon at Pentecost, he was telling the people of Israel exactly who Jesus was, and as he was finishing up, this is what happened...Acts 2:36-37 says, "Therefore let all the house of Israel know assuredly, that God hath made that same Jesus, WHOM YE HAVE CRUCIFIED, both Lord and Christ (THE MESSAGE). Now when they heard this, THEY WERE PRICKED IN THEIR HEART (CONVICTION), and said unto Peter and to the rest of the apostles, Men and brethren, WHAT SHALL WE DO?"...OH MY!! They were HUMBLE, they were CONTRITE, they were REPENTANT, and they wanted to know WHAT SHALL WE DO to make it right!! They CHOSE CONVERSION or CHANGE!!

Later, Peter and the apostles were brought before the council for teaching in Jesus' name after they had been ordered not to...this is how they answered...Acts 5:29-33 says, "Then Peter and the other apostles answered and said, We ought to obey God rather than men. The God of our fathers raised up Jesus, WHOM YE SLEW and hanged on a tree. Him hath God exalted with his right hand to be a Prince and a Savior, for to give repentance to Israel, and forgiveness of sins. And we are his witnesses of these things; and so is also the Holy Ghost, whom God hath given to them that obey him (THE MESSAGE). When they heard that, THEY WERE CUT TO THE HEART (CONVICTION), and took counsel to slay them"...BAD BAD BAD!!

These men were made to KNOW that they were wrong—they even FELT IT—but they CHOSE NOT TO CHANGE!!

OH LORD!! When we are made to KNOW, and made to FEEL conviction, help us ALWAYS to CHOOSE TO CHANGE!! In Jesus' Name.

Daily Instructions

Someone very close to me had recently been delivered of demonic possession. As she was still struggling with the whole days-long event, I felt to give her these instructions for her personal daily reminders.

These were personally for her, but maybe helpful for someone else...

-Please try to carefully observe all of these daily in your walk.

-Do not use profanity, no matter how innocent it may seem.

-Do not ask a single question when someone is telling you about someone else's business, no matter how "interesting" it is, no matter how badly you want to know more details.

-Do not repeat anyone else's business, whether the subject comes up or not, or whether it is true information or not.

-Do not talk about anyone's past failures. You don't know whether or not they have been bloodbought. You, nor anyone else, has the right, the authority, nor the ability to drag someone else's things out from under the blood of Jesus. And it is not your business.

-If you start thinking something "unflattering" about anyone, or yourself, start praying for them and for yourself, and even sing praises to God.

-Make it a point to read the Bible every day. Do not skip a day. Begin in Genesis. Anything else anyone tells you to read or anything else you feel to read other than "where your bookmark is" should be extra for the day. Read it too.

-When anyone "attacks" you, no matter how minor or how big, bite your tongue. Speak softly and with a positive response, when possible. This is important. It will most likely happen often.

-Do not lie. Even and especially when telling the truth will be more uncomfortable than telling the lie.

-Be as fair as possible in everything you say and do.

*All of the above instructions include text messaging.

-Verbally thank God every day for each and every blessing and gift and lesson in your life that you can think of.

-Pray as often as you can every day.

-Assemble with other true believers as much as possible.

-Purposely try to not be offended when someone says or thinks anything "unflattering" about you. Remember, it is only "their bad" until it makes you mad, then it is yours too.

-Remind yourself daily OR MORE that you are not damned or hopeless. You are still alive. This also goes for every living person.

-Separate the person from the sin. If someone does something that is hurtful to you, you still have to love that person as well as forgive them. You hate the sin, not the person.

-If there comes a time when you are dragged into "drama" or have difficult feelings toward someone else, it is extremely important to NOT involve another person by telling them about the issues that made you mad. This could cause them to have difficult feelings for someone when they weren't even involved in the incident.

-Pay attention. Pray and ask God to help you to see what goes on around you every day in the spiritual realm. The things that you can see going on around you every day are nothing compared to the things that you can't see. It takes God opening your spiritual eyes and you being willing to pay attention.

Don't Tempt Me 1

Where does temptation come from? Do you say, "Well the devil, of course"?

To tempt is to induce or entice a person to sin, to arouse desire in, to attract.

James 1:13 says, "Let no man say when he is tempted, I am tempted of God: for God cannot be tempted with evil, neither tempteth he any man:"

Well, it doesn't come from God, so...

Temptation is defined as inner pressure caused by interaction of circumstances AND the limitations that are qualities of our humanity itself.

James 1:14 goes on to say, "But every man is tempted, when he is drawn away of his own lust (desires), and enticed"...uh oh...this doesn't sound like we can blame it all on the devil either.

Now, Ephesians 6:16 tells us, "Above all, taking the shield of faith, wherewith ye shall be able to quench all the FIERY DARTS of the wicked"...this is what part the enemy has in it. He sees a potential situation and he fires a dart at us. BUT we can't blame it all on him. That's what he does.

"Often the temptation situation itself is not evil; the evil lies within us."

PROCEED WITH CAUTION!!

This is about to get personal. Take the fiery dart of jealousy, for example. Jealousy is defined as envy stimulated by a desire for something that rightly belongs to another. If I have the gift of the word of Knowledge and you don't, but you have the gift of Interpretation and I don't, the enemy sees that situation as an opening to fire a dart of jealousy AT BOTH OF US!!

BUT, 1 Corinthians 12:11 says, "But all these worketh that one and the selfsame Spirit, dividing to every man severally as He will."

This tells me that there is no reason for me to be jealous of you or for you to be jealous of me, because God decides which person operates with which gift. AND WE ALL BENEFIT FROM IT!! I am thankful for whatever He would have me do. I am also thankful for whatever He would have you do. PRAISE THE LORD!!

Don't throw the towel in yet though, there is hope. "When we are attracted to wrong, we have the opportunity to CHOOSE what is right and so be strengthened Spiritually." WOW!! IT'S OUR CHOICE!!

1 Corinthians 10:13 says, "There hath no temptation taken you but such as is common to man: but God is faithful, who will not suffer you to be tempted above that ye are able; but will with the temptation (which, remember does NOT come from Him) also make A WAY TO ESCAPE, that ye may be able to bear it." OH, MY GOODNESS!! THANK YOU, JESUS!!

So the situation arises, the enemy fires his dart, BUT...GOD makes a way for us to escape, GOD gives us the opportunity, wisdom, and knowledge to CHOOSE to avoid falling into that temptation!!

It isn't like a maze where we have to search for the exit...ALL WE HAVE TO DO IS KNOW THAT IT'S THERE!! AND IT IS!! EVERY TIME!! PRAISE GOD!!

Don't Tempt Me 2

Continued...

When a temptation situation arises, the enemy fires his dart (whether it's a dart of jealousy or some other kind), then GOD makes a way for us to escape, and GOD gives us the opportunity, wisdom, and knowledge to CHOOSE to avoid falling into that temptation. It is OUR CHOICE.

Because the evil lies within US. So who among us can be tempted?

James 1:14 says that EVERY man is tempted...Well, not me, I'm too close to God...READ CAREFULLY...getting personal again.

I can't be enticed to sin, I'm the song leader, temptation won't touch me. I'm a Sunday School teacher, I read the Bible and pray every day, or I AM THE PASTOR, or I've been a Christian for 30 years!!

Well, Galatians 6:1 says, "Brethren, if a man be overtaken in a fault, ye which are spiritual, restore such a one in the spirit of meekness; considering thyself, lest thou also be tempted." OH NO!! "ye which are spiritual" can be tempted too!!

Matthew 23:12 says, "And whosoever shall exalt himself shall be abased; and he that shall humble himself shall be exalted."

Not only does this tell us that if you have yourself lifted up above the possibility of temptation in your own mind, YOU MAY have to prove that!! And you MAY NOT pass that test!! But, it also tells us that if, in your own mind, you are humble enough to admit that you need prayer and God and help to avoid falling into temptation, chances are you WILL have the help you need to get through temptation victoriously. THANK GOD FOR HUMILITY!!

Romans 12:3 says, "For I say, through the grace given to me, to every man that is among you, not to think of himself more highly than he ought to think; but to think SOBERLY (DO NOT BECOME INTOXICATED WITH YOUR OWN SELF), according as God hath dealt to EVERY man the measure of faith."

So whoever you may be, or whatever position you may hold, do not think that you are above the possibility of temptation OR the possibility of falling into it. ALSO, don't be the one that thinks that you are the only one who struggles and needs help. WE ALL...EVERYONE is tempted and not above falling.

Even the Hard Ones

As Christians, filled with the Holy Spirit, we are required to minister to people who do not know the Lord. Some of us minister as circumstances, situations, or opportunities are presented. Others are in "full-time" ministry, where they minister usually to a specific group of individuals. These may include teenagers, married couples, children, recovering addicts, victims of domestic violence, or some other group of people.

This particular lesson came to me in reference to the ones who minister to the groups of people that have had a less-than-easy background. The groups who may be difficult to minister to.

I have witnessed, and been a part of one of these places that minister to this group of people. I learned that there are individuals that are easy to minister to, as well as the ones that you struggle to endure. I know that sounds horrible. But, it is the truth.

The difficult ones are not always of the same mind that we are. By that I mean that they would sometimes rather continue on the road to destruction, for whatever reason. Whether they have come from a broken home, prison, drug addiction, or something equally potentially devastating.

The road that they have been travelling is familiar to them. Sometimes it's just easier for them to stay on that road than it is to admit that they need to change their direction.

But, this isn't really about them, it's about us, the ones who are supposed to be there to minister to them.

John 13:1 says, "Now before the feast of the passover, when Jesus knew that his hour was come that he should depart out of this world unto the Father, having loved his own which were in the world, HE LOVED THEM UNTO THE END."

2- "And supper being ended, the devil having now put into the heart of Judas Iscariot, Simon's son, to betray him;"

11- "For he knew who should betray him; therefore said he, Ye are not all clean."

21- "When Jesus had thus said, he was troubled in spirit, and testified, and said, Verily, verily, I say unto you, that one of you shall betray me."

23- "Now there was leaning on Jesus' bosom one of his disciples, whom Jesus loved."

26- "Jesus answered, He it is, to whom I shall give a sop, when I have dipped it. And when he had dipped the sop, he gave it to Judas Iscariot, the son of Simon."

We know that it was "John the Beloved" who leaned on Jesus' bosom. We also know that Jesus loved him. He would have been one of the easy ones to minister to.

But Judas Iscariot, who Jesus KNEW was about to betray Him, JESUS LOVED HIM UNTO THE END, TOO! He dipped the bread and gave it to him to eat! KNOWING what Judas was about to do!

If we are in the position to minister to any particular group of people, we MUST minister to and LOVE the hard ones, UNTO THE END! What is our reward if we only minister to the easy ones? LORD, HELP US!!

Exhorting One Another

Hebrews 10:25 says, "Not forsaking the assembling of ourselves together, as the manner of some is; but exhorting one another: and so much the more, as ye see the day approaching."

I can't tell you how many times I have heard someone preach and teach from this particular verse of Scripture, or how many times I've referred to it myself, trying to "quote Scripture" to someone in order to convince them that the "right" or "required" thing for them to do is GO TO CHURCH!!

Because that's what it says, "not forsaking the assembling of ourselves together". Well, NOW I can see the middle part of that verse, THANK YOU, LORD!! And for whatever reason, I don't remember ever having heard a lesson or message on it before.

It says, "as the manner of some is; but exhorting one another:"

Apparently, there were some who were forsaking the assembling of themselves together in the early church, for whatever reason...DO YOU SEE ANY OF THAT TODAY?? YES!! And what do we do about it??

We act like they have something CONTAGEOUS, and we stay away from them?? We TALK ABOUT them?? We look at them like they are UNCLEAN?? We treat them like GARBAGE!!

We can, right?? Because we still go to church and they don't, right?? WRONG!! This verse commands us to NOT forsake the assembling of ourselves together, EVEN THOUGH THERE ARE SOME THAT HAVE DONE JUST THAT...but next, it commands us to do something else...EXHORT ONE ANOTHER!! OH, MY GOODNESS!!

To exhort means to urge or ask earnestly, to beseech, to entreat, to implore, and OH MY!! to cry out and to beg!! OH LORD MY GOD!! FORGIVE ME FORGIVE ME FORGIVE ME..I have not done this the right way!!

It says…"and so much the more, as ye see the day approaching"…WE KNOW THAT WE KNOW THAT WE KNOW that we are living in the last of days, the signs are EVERYWHERE!! I heard someone say it best last night, "We are living on borrowed time!"

We are supposed to be CRYING OUT AND BEGGING people not only to COME to God, but we are supposed to be CRYING OUT AND BEGGING people to STAY with God!! TO COME BACK TO GOD!!

I had 2 whole pages of notes that I wrote on this subject after the Lord gave it to me. I don't believe I need them now. The only other point I need to make is this…

Hebrews 12:1b says, "and let us run with patience the race that is set before us."

Hebrews 11:39-40 says this- "And these all, having obtained a good report through faith,

RECEIVED NOT THE PROMISE: God having provided some better thing for us, THAT THEY

WITHOUT US SHOULD NOT BE MADE PERFECT."

We are all going to FINISH this race together!! By this, I mean, one person doesn't get a crown and the rest of us get an honorable mention. If we run this race AS INSTRUCTED IN THE WORD, WE ALL GET THE CROWN!! And if I think I am "going too fast" for my brother or sister to keep up, or if they are about to give up, OH MY!! I had better go to CRYING OUT AND BEGGING THEM not to give up!! I should want them to get their crown as much as I want mine!!

Face to Face

Have you ever tried to think of a word or phrase for days without success? Like when you are trying to think of the person's name who sings a particular song? Oh, it will drive you crazy!

Well, for me, it happened to be a two-word phrase. I thought about it for days. I could describe what the phrase was referring to. But, no one seemed to know what I was talking about.

And when it FINALLY came to me, I WAS SO EXCITED!! It may sound silly, but I just KNEW there was a phrase for what I was trying so hard to describe...

Have you ever watched one of those "medieval" movies where there is a king and queen who live in a castle and "runs" a "kingdom"? And when one of the "common" people in their kingdom has an issue to discuss with the king or queen, they may have to make an appointment to "see" them?

The phrase that I could not think of was describing the intention of the person who wanted to see the king or queen...they were "SEEKING AUDIENCE" with the king or queen!

To seek audience with someone means that you seek them until you find them! Did you get that?? You seek to be FACE TO FACE with someone and you seek until you find!

It came to me like this...You are seeking audience with the king or queen. You want to be face to face with them. First, you must go through the gates. Next, you have to pass through their courts, outer and inner. Then, you enter into the throne room, and you are face to face with them.

So, here we go...

1 Chronicles 16:11 says, "Seek the Lord and his strength, seek his face continually."

Psalm 100:4 says, "Enter into his gates with thanksgiving, and into his courts with praise: be thankful unto him, and bless his name."

OH, MY MY MY!!! If you have an issue that you need to discuss with the Lord, you need to be "seeking audience" with Him! You need to be FACE TO FACE with Him!

How do we do that?? We enter into His gates with thanksgiving, and into His courts with praise!!

First, we must pass through His gates, then His courts. We are to PRAISE our way through these in order to enter into THE THRONE ROOM!!

I am thankful Lord! I praise You Lord! Help me to never fail to be thankful for all You have done concerning me! In Jesus' Name.

Found Wanting

I woke up during the night with the phrase "found wanting" repeating over and over in my mind.

As I began to study this phrase, I could not have imagined all that I would learn.

Wanting means lacking in a certain required or necessary quality; not supplied.

The word "found" has more than one meaning.

#1-having been discovered by chance or unexpectedly.

#2-to take the first steps in building.

First, when you hear "found wanting", it makes you afraid that the Lord is going to "FIND" you LACKING something that is REQUIRED by Him. And this is true. It can mean just that. None of us want that.

But...

Found is the root word for foundation. A foundation is an underlying basis or principle.

Matthew 7:24-27 says, "Therefore whosoever heareth these sayings of mine, and doeth them, I will liken him unto a wise man, which built his house upon a rock: And the rain descended, and the floods came, and the winds blew, and beat upon that house; and it fell not: for it was founded upon a rock. And every one that heareth these sayings of mine, and doeth them not, shall be likened unto a foolish man, which built his house upon the sand: And the rain descended, and the floods came, and the winds blew, and beat upon that house; and it fell: and great was the fall of it."

In this passage, the wise man who built his house upon a rock made sure his FOUNDATION WASN'T LACKING. The foolish man who built his house upon the sand did not. He was FOUND WANTING. His foundation was lacking.

So, what does this mean?

1 Corinthians 3:11 says, "For other foundation can no man lay than that is laid, which is Jesus Christ."

If our underlying basis or principle, or our foundation, is not Jesus Christ, we will be FOUND WANTING. Our "house" will fall.

Last but certainly not least, the enemy would have us to believe that we will be "found wanting", but in a completely different way.

With wanting meaning lacking, he would have us to believe that we LACK; healing, deliverance, salvation, provision, peace, victory, restoration, and so on.

Psalm 23:1 says, "The Lord is my shepherd; I SHALL NOT WANT."

Lord, I thank You that my foundation is laid on Jesus Christ, the only sure foundation. Help me to not be lacking anything that You require when You "find" me. Also, help me to remember that I shall not lack any good thing as long as You are my Shepherd, in Jesus' Name.

Get Busy

Do we know when we are in the place God has put us? Do we do the things that we KNOW we are supposed to do and then pray to be led and given guidance by the Spirit to find out the rest?

And then, do we do according to what we are instructed to do by the Spirit? Or do we drag our feet? In 2 Chronicles 29, we are told that at age 25, Hezekiah began to reign as King of Judah, and he did that which was right in the sight of the Lord.

2 Chronicles 29:3-5 says, "He IN THE FIRST YEAR of his reign, IN THE FIRST MONTH, opened the doors of the house of the Lord, and repaired them. And he brought in the priests and the Levites, and gathered them together into the east street, And said unto them, Hear me, ye Levites, sanctify now yourselves, and sanctify the house of the Lord God of your fathers, and carry forth the filthiness out of the holy place."

Then verse 17a says, "now they began ON THE FIRST DAY OF THE FIRST MONTH to sanctify, and on the eighth day of the month came they to the porch of the Lord: so they sanctified the house of the Lord in eight days;"

DID YOU SEE THAT!?! In the FIRST YEAR, in the FIRST MONTH, on the FIRST DAY, Hezekiah got busy!

Before Hezekiah was anointed King, he apparently didn't have the authority to do what he knew was the right thing to do. He wasn't in the PLACE to do it, to make the changes that needed to be made. BUT when he became King, IN THE FIRST YEAR, IN THE FIRST MONTH, ON THE FIRST DAY, he began to do what he was

ANOINTED and APPOINTED to do. Hezekiah DID NOT waste any time!!

So, if we know we are where God has placed us, then we know He has NOT put us there to do NOTHING! We have a job to do! Let's NOT waste time! Let's get busy!

Lord, help me today to do EVERYTHING You have created, called, chosen, anointed, and appointed me to do. I DO NOT want to waste Your time. Enlighten my understanding if I don't know all of my calling and appointment. Equip and enable me to GET BUSY!! In Jesus' Name.

He Is Not Random

As I was reading in Genesis and Exodus, I made notes in the margin of my Bible to "study this", in reference to a couple of different verses.

The first one, Genesis 46:34 says, "That ye shall say, Thy servants' trade hath been about cattle from our youth even until now, both we, and also our fathers: that ye may dwell in the land of Goshen; for every shepherd is an abomination unto the Egyptians."

The second one, Exodus 12:12 says, "For I will pass through the land of Egypt this night, and will smite all the first-born in the land of Egypt, both man and beast; and against all the gods of Egypt I will execute judgment: I am the Lord."

The children of Israel were to tell Pharaoh that they all were, and had been for generations, shepherds. "Every shepherd" was an abomination to the Egyptians. The Egyptians hated shepherds!

I was curious as to why the Egyptians hated shepherds. I found out that and more!

In the second verse above, God said, "against all the gods of Egypt I will execute judgment:" I started to look to see what I could find out about Egyptian gods and goddesses.

First of all, there were ten plagues that the Lord sent against Egypt. The number 10 represents fullness of quantity. Ten Egyptian plagues meant that Egypt was completely and fully plagued.

Egyptian god	Plague
Hapi-god of the Nile	Water turned to blood
Heket-head of a frog-goddess of fertility	Plague of frogs
Geb-god of the Earth	Dust became lice
Khepri-head of a fly-god of creation	Swarms of flies
Hathor-head of a cow-goddess of protection	Death of cattle and livestock
Isis-goddess of medicine and peace	Ashes turned to boils and sores
Nut-goddess of the sky	Hail rained down as fire
Seth-god of storms and disorder	Locusts sent from the sky
Ra-the sun god	Three days of complete darkness
Pharaoh-the ultimate power of Egypt	Death of the firstborn

GOD DID EXECUTE JUDGMENT AGAINST THE EGYPTIAN GODS! These plagues WERE NOT random! OUR GOD IS NOT RANDOM! PRAISE THE LORD!

Now, as to the shepherds being an abomination unto the Egyptians, the children of Israel sacrificed animals to GOD that the Egyptians considered gods. I imagine the Egyptians did hate that!

Lord, I thank You for showing me these things in Your Word. I thank You that You are purposeful about Your children and not random. You are also the only God who can and does protect His children. Thank you, Lord.

He Loves me

I am so awed by the fact that God loves me...

Psalm 139:1 says, "O Lord, thou hast searched me, and known me."

Now, we know that He knows us, and we are so quick to quote Scripture that reminds us that He knows us, inside and out. BUT, His Word says that He has SEARCHED me. To search is something that is done ON PURPOSE!!

Search means to look for something concealed, to diligently look for, to probe.

It also says He has KNOWN me. To know is to be well-informed about, to KNOW something is to have it securely in the memory, in the mind!! WOW!!

This passage of Scripture through the next 2 verses expounds upon the first verse...it says, "Thou knowest my downsitting and mine uprising, thou understandest my thought afar off. Thou compassest my path and my lying down, and art acquainted with all my ways."

He knows when I am sitting down, when I am getting up, and He understands my thoughts, the way I reason things out, any idea I may have, He knows and understands it...EVEN WHEN I DON'T!! He compasses my path and my lying down...He surrounds my path (every step I take),

AND HE FENCES ME IN WHEN I AM LYING DOWN!! OH, MY GOODNESS!! He is acquainted with ALL my ways!!

Sometimes I don't even know what I'm doing, so I can say that even I am not acquainted with all my ways. So, when I say that I am so awed by the fact that God loves me, I mean just that!!

Please know that this is for you, too!!

Help Me Lord

I have heard as long as I can remember that "prayer changes things". I don't EVEN like the fact that I have to say this, but here goes...

I was skeptical. I guess the thing was that when I wanted results right then, I didn't want to take the time to pray, let alone wait for an answer. BUT, I have come to know that PRAYER is the ONLY way to get the RIGHT answer, when it is the RIGHT TIME for the answer. THANK YOU, LORD!

After pondering and meditating about this, by the help of the Lord, I have come to realize something else about myself. I was hesitant to pray because of the person I was. I knew what kind of person I was, and I was just ABSOLUTELY POSITIVE that God WOULD NOT do anything I asked Him to do. So my mentality was, "why pray?"

I know now that, for a time, this mentality followed me into my relationship with Him. I knew I had to pray. I knew I needed to pray. I knew there were issues in my life that demanded that I pray. BUT, I COULD NOT bring myself to do it. And to pray for someone else? Forget it! I felt like it would do more harm than good. I felt that I had no business praying for ANYBODY. But I remember going to bed night after night, and as I would lay my head on my pillow, I would just whisper, "help me Lord".

Now, with tears streaming down my face, I have to take the time to thank Him. HE HEARD ME even when all I could say was "help me Lord." THANK YOU, LORD, FOR TAKING THE TIME FOR SOMEONE LIKE ME!! To know that He actually listens to me when I talk. WOW!!

And how COMPLETELY HUMBLING to realize that He was listening even then! I have also learned that praying for myself, although needed, is NOT all I am called to do.

James 5:16 says, "Confess your faults one to another, AND PRAY ONE FOR ANOTHER, that YE may be healed"...OH MY GOODNESS!! Did you see that?? YOU pray for one another that YOU may be healed!! YES!! That's what it says! And I can tell you personally, that prayers I pray for someone else, are being answered for myself as well. Now look at the second part of that verse.

"The effectual fervent (earnest, sincere) prayer of a righteous man AVAILETH MUCH"...WOW!! It doesn't just say that the prayer he prays is answered...it says that that prayer AVAILETH MUCH!!

"Availeth much" means accomplishing a great or outstanding amount. I know SOME of what God has done for me, in me, through me, and around me. I am SURE I don't know ALL He has done. But, I do know that He has gone WELL ABOVE AND BEYOND what I have EVER deserved. Not to mention, what I ever expected or imagined when I whispered every night, "help me Lord." THANK YOU, JESUS!! Thank you for being patient with me. Thank You for doing things in me that I wasn't aware I even needed. Thank You for changing me. I ask that You continue to transform me into ALL that You created, and have called and chosen me to be, in Jesus' Name.

Hold Them Up

In Exodus 17, the Amalekites came and fought against the children of Israel. Verse 11 says,

"And it came to pass, when Moses held up his hand, that Israel prevailed: and when he let down his hand, Amalek prevailed."

We need to understand that when one side prevailed, the other side suffered losses...PEOPLE DIED!! As long as Moses' hand was up, Israel prevailed. But, when Moses' hand was down, Israel suffered losses...PEOPLE DIED!!

Verse 12 says, "But Moses' hands were heavy; and they took a stone, and put it under him, and he sat thereon; and Aaron and Hur stayed up his hands, the one on the one side, and the other on the other side; and his hands were steady until the going down of the sun."

DID YOU SEE THAT!?! Moses' hands were heavy, and he had to have help to hold them up so that Israel PREVAILED!! Moses was the leader, and when his hands grew heavy so that he could no longer hold them up himself, other members of the CONGREGATION of the children of Israel had to help hold his hands up so that they would not SUFFER LOSSES!!

Lord, I pray that You help each one of us to do our part in holding up the hands of our leaders.

Help us to surround them and cover them in prayer every day BEFORE the possibility of suffering losses becomes a reality. Help us to not look on this need as a weakness in leadership, but enable us to look on them with Your love and compassion, knowing that they carry the greater burden, in Jesus' Name.

Hold Whatcha Got!

If you have had to hold a board for someone to put a nail in it, or if you have had to hold onto one end of the tape measure for someone else to mark the board on the other end, then chances are, you have heard this before.

"Hold whatcha got!" It means don't move. Don't let it slip. Don't drop it.

Something I read in the Word reminded me of this phrase.

Philippians 3:12-16 says, "Not as though I had already attained, either were already perfect: but I follow after, if that I may apprehend that for which also I am apprehended of Christ Jesus.

Brethren, I count not myself to have apprehended: but this one thing I do, forgetting those things which are behind, and reaching forth unto those things which are before, I press toward the mark for the prize of the high calling of God in Christ Jesus. Let us therefore, as many as be perfect, be thus minded: and if in any thing ye be otherwise minded, God shall reveal even this unto you.

Nevertheless, whereto we have already attained, let us walk by the same rule, let us mind the same thing."

In this passage, Paul is telling the church at Philippi that he does not consider himself perfect.

But, he is following after perfection. Forgetting his past faults and failures, he is perfectly PRESSING forward.

"Nevertheless, whereto we have already attained, let us walk by the same rule, let us mind the same thing."

This means, HOLD WHATCHA GOT! DON'T LET IT SLIP! DON'T DROP IT!

If you don't think you have advanced in your walk with the Lord as much as you should have, or if you look at others and think that they are way ahead of you, HOLD WHATCHA GOT! DO NOT GIVE UP!

We are to keep going. Press toward the mark for the prize. It doesn't matter if you seem to be moving slow or slower than others. The main thing is to keep moving.

Some may seem to be running. Some may seem to be jogging. Some may seem to be speed walking. While you feel like you are crawling. DO NOT STOP!

Revelation 3:11 says, "Behold, I come quickly: HOLD THAT FAST WHICH THOU HAST, that no man take thy crown."

None of us have made it yet. We all have "slow" days. Some days even seem to be completely "unproductive". But, hold on to where you have made it so far. DON'T LET IT SLIP! DON'T DROP IT! HOLD WHATCHA GOT!

Lord, if anyone ever feels like quitting because they have not made enough "progress" in their walk with You, I ask that You help me to encourage them to hold on to the progress they have made. I also ask that if I ever find myself of the mind to give up, You send someone to encourage me, in Jesus' Name.

Humility or Humiliation

Do you know there is a big difference between humility and humiliation?

Humility is a modest or low view of one's own importance; humbleness.

Humiliation is the action of humiliating someone; the state of being humiliated.

Humiliate means to make someone feel ashamed and foolish by injuring their dignity and selfrespect, especially publicly; to reduce someone to a lower position in one's own eyes or in the eyes of others.

Humility is something that comes from within and is required in order to serve the Lord.

Humiliation on the other hand, comes from without, from someone else. This often happens when one person tries to make another person look bad so that they themselves will look better in others' eyes. This is not required. It also is NOT of God.

Proverbs 16:18-19 says, "Pride goeth before destruction, and an haughty spirit before a fall.

Better it is to be of an humble spirit with the lowly, than to divide the spoil with the proud."

This tells me that if you go out of your way to cause someone else's humiliation in order to make yourself look better than them, you are prideful, your destruction is approaching, you will soon fall, and you should have been satisfied with the way things were. Because the spoil (your reward) will not be a benefit to you.

James 4:6 says, "But he giveth more grace. Wherefore he saith, God resisteth the proud, but giveth grace unto the humble."

We see the perfect picture of this in John 8:1-11 when the Pharisees brought unto Jesus a woman taken in adultery. They sought to humiliate her, even to have her stoned. But Jesus resisted their pride, and granted grace unto her. They didn't leave with satisfaction, but conviction. She didn't leave with condemnation, but grace.

Lord, I thank You for humility. I ask that You guard me against a prideful and haughty spirit.

Forgive me when I stumble. Help me to never try to humiliate anyone, but to extend grace to them, the same grace You have extended to me, in Jesus' Name.

I Am Redeemed

What does it actually mean to be redeemed?

Redeem means to trade for something (or someone).

Luke 1:68 says, "Blessed be the Lord God of Israel; for he hath visited and redeemed his people,"

God has redeemed us...

WOW!! HIS THOUGHTS REALLY ARE NOT OUR THOUGHTS AND HIS WAYS ARE NOT OUR WAYS!!

We trade cars, right? I go to look at or VISIT a car to trade mine in for. Usually the one I am using to trade IN is in worse shape than the one I am trading FOR. I am essentially trading IN a "hunk of junk" FOR something that is actually BETTER, something that will not have to be worked on, something I can depend on. Something that will do what it's supposed to do when it's supposed to do it. Right?

Well, that is the way WE do it. But God, came to look at, or VISIT, me. He knew what kind of shape I was in. He traded His only begotten Son, Who was PERFECT, for me. A "hunk of junk" that He knew He would ALWAYS have to work on!!

Lord, I thank You, thank You, thank You that You redeemed me! I thank You for ALWAYS working on me!

In a Strait

I was thinking about the words to the song, Beulah Land. "I'm kind of homesick for a country, to which I've never been before...Beulah Land, I'm longing for you, and some day, on thee I'll stand, and there my home shall be eternal...I'm looking out across the river, where my faith will end in sight, there's just a few more days to labor"...OH MY!

Do you know this made me think of something Paul said?

Philippians 1:21-24 says, "For to me to live is Christ, and to die is gain. But if I live in the flesh, this is the fruit of my labor: YET WHAT I SHALL CHOOSE I WOT NOT. FOR I AM IN A STRAIT BETWIXT TWO, having a desire to depart, and to be with Christ; which is far better:

Nevertheless to abide in the flesh is more needful for you."

Are we in a place where we truly DESIRE TO DEPART??? Do we KNOW which one we would choose? Would it be a difficult decision? And would we only choose to "abide in the flesh" to benefit others???

Could we turn loose of our lives and all that they entail? Our plans? Our homes? Our wealth?

Our families? Our children? Or would we steadily be looking back, like Lot's wife? OH MY!! Lord, help me to DESIRE to be with You more than I desire ANYTHING else. Enable me to LONG for that Land. Help us all, Lord, to come to a place in our walk with You, that we don't have a single dread or worry about what we would be leaving behind, in Jesus' Name.

Invitation Only

Doubt, you're not allowed here—Fear, you have no place

Shame, you're not invited—Mercy filled your space

Bitterness, you may go now—Unforgiveness, you take heed

Resentment, anger, hurt, and strife, you no more I need

Because my walk from here on out will be by invitation only

I will take the gifts and grace given by the One that bought me

From this point forward, past mistakes won't bind me anymore

So I will tell you one last time, go now, there's the door

Pride, I won't be needing you—I am all I need to be

Lies, you are mistaken, if you think you are believed

Jealous envy, Jesus gives me everything I need

So, all of you, get up and go, you're no longer leading me

Rejection, you have nearly taken all my self-esteem

But now, I am rejecting you, I'm telling you to leave

I know that I'm just what the Lord intended me to be

I'm good enough, I'm strong enough, just watch and you will see

Because my walk from here on out will be by invitation only

I will take the gifts and grace given by the One that bought me

From this point forward, past mistakes won't bind me anymore

So I will tell you one last time, go now, there's the door

It Is Possible

Have you ever had so great a need that, when you prayed, you only asked God for "half of it"?

Whether it was a financial need, a need for healing, or some other kind of need? Maybe you needed or wanted your situation to work out in a certain way, but you didn't see any way that it ever could. So, you didn't pray about it in that way. Maybe you thought it was "too much to ask".

I need to stop right here to address a very specific NEED.

Salvation. If you think that you are so far into sin or that you have denied or neglected the Lord for so long that you could never be saved, YOU CAN!

Matthew 19:25-26 says, "When his disciples heard it, they were exceedingly amazed, saying,

Who then can be saved? But Jesus beheld them, and said unto them, With men this is impossible; but with God all things are possible."

Possible means able to be done. YOU CAN BE SAVED!

Luke 1:37 says, "For with God nothing shall be impossible."

Impossible means not able to occur, exist, or be done. If we don't know something exists, how are we to ask for it? But God can do even those things!

Ephesians 3:20 says, "Now unto him that is able to do exceeding abundantly above all that we ask or think, according to the power that worketh in us."

DON'T PUT LIMITS ON GOD!! He is able to do EXCEEDING ABUNDANTLY more than you could ever even think to ask Him for! Whatever or however great your need may be, with GOD, IT IS POSSIBLE!

It's Our Responsibility

I recently watched a video. In the video, a black man was being held down on the ground by a white man, who was a law enforcement officer. The video also showed other officers standing by, attempting to subdue the crowd of onlookers. The black man was held down on the ground until he died.

This was a horrible event. The video was difficult to watch. I felt so bad for the man who died. It was heartbreaking. I wanted to hate the man who held him down. I was also certain that the stand-by officers could have done something differently. And the onlookers, why didn't they do something? But then I am reminded that...

Romans 8:28 says, "And we know that all things work together for good to them that love God, to them who are the called according to his purpose."

Even if a situation is orchestrated by the enemy of our souls, God will work it together for our good! If we receive and allow Him to show us how!

This event on video for the whole world to see gave the enemy the perfect opportunity to scream, "BLACK AGAINST WHITE" and "CITIZEN AGAINST LAW ENFORCEMENT". He DID NOT miss that opportunity! And we took the bait! Our entire nation has been turned into a battleground!

Then the Lord showed me what I had actually seen in that video.

The Lord began by telling me that many of His people have been in the position of the man on the ground, even myself. Many of His people have been in the position of the man who held him down, even myself. Many of His people have been in the position of the stand-by officers, even myself. And many of His people have been in the position of the onlookers, even myself. IN THE CHURCH!!

How many times does a brother or sister-in-Christ stumble, and instead of helping them up, we hold them down? Do we hold them down, in their time of trouble, until the whole world sees?

Do we make sure they know that everyone has witnessed their moment of weakness. If we do eventually help them up, do they even have the will to keep fighting this fight, knowing that everyone saw their failure? Some of us may have even orchestrated it! Or do we hold them down, even unto death? OH LORD MY GOD!!

The Lord showed me that just as I watched that video, the world is watching the church. I SAID,

THE WORLD IS WATCHING THE CHURCH!!

AND WHAT DO THEY SEE!?!

Yes, they see the Church warring among ourselves...warring against one another...fighting over positions...writhing with jealousy toward one another...full of envy and strife and backbiting and criticism and judgment...assembly against assembly...member against member... holding one another down, even unto death!

I have seen a variety of suggestions on social media and the news as to how to remedy the current state of our nation, our land. But, there is only one.

2 Chronicles 7:14 says, "If my people, which are called by my name, shall humble themselves, and pray, and seek my face, and turn from their wicked ways; then will I hear from heaven, and will forgive their sin, and will heal their land."

It is OUR responsibility, our duty, to change the way the world sees the Church! If watching the Church is no different than watching the world, why are we inviting them in? Why would they want to come in?

Lord, I thank You for helping me to see this through Your eyes. I ask that You help me to always help a brother or sister up if they stumble, and never hold them down. Your Word says that a just man falls seven times and rises again. I ask You to enable me to give them aid and encouragement. I also ask that You protect me from those who would hold me down if I stumble.

Lord, help Your Church to change the way we need to in order to be what we are supposed to be to the world and to glorify You, in Jesus' Name.

It's Time to Grow

--I had a dream, and I don't remember much about the dream except, a woman, I don't know who she was, took hold of both sides of my head and leaned close to my face and said "it's time to grow".

--In the same dream it seemed, someone (I guess it was the same woman) was introducing me to an older lady that I would need to speak with before I left whatever place I was in, in the dream.

--I hope this will make sense by the time I'm done.

So, with the words "it's time to grow" in mind, I started studying. This is what I found...

Ecclesiastes 3:1 says "To every thing there is a season, and A TIME TO EVERY PURPOSE under the heaven:"

Grow- means to advance, to improve, to make progress, to progress to maturity.

Regarding maturity, I thought about the older lady in the dream that I was introduced to.

Titus 2:3-5 says

"The aged women likewise, that they be in behaviour as becometh holiness (holy women), not false accusers (troublemakers), not given to much wine, teachers of good things; That they may teach the young women to be sober (wise), to love their husbands, to love their children, To be discreet, chaste, keepers at home, good, obedient to their own husbands, that the word of God be not blasphemed."

It is from the elders that the younger generation is to learn the way to become and to be holy.

1 Peter 2:2 says "As newborn babes, desire the sincere milk of the word, that ye may grow thereby:"

Hebrews 5:13-14 says, "For every one that useth milk is unskilful in the word of righteousness: for he is a babe." But strong meat belongeth to them that are of full age, even those who BY REASON OF USE have their SENSES EXERCISED TO DISCERN both good and evil."

*practice to discern

2 Peter 3:18 says "But grow in grace, and in the knowledge of our Lord and Saviour Jesus Christ.

To him be glory both now and for ever. Amen."

Proverbs 4:5-9 says "Get wisdom, get understanding: forget it not; neither decline from the words of my mouth. Forsake her not, and she shall preserve thee: love her, and she shall keep thee. Wisdom is the principal thing; therefore get wisdom: and with all thy getting get understanding. Exalt her, and she shall promote thee: she shall bring thee to honour, when thou dost embrace her. She shall give to thine head an ornament of grace: a crown of glory shall she deliver to thee."

Proverbs 2:4-5 says "If thou seekest her as silver, and searchest for her as for hid treasures; Then shalt thou understand the fear of the Lord, and find the knowledge of God."

So, how do we grow? We grow up physically. We grow educationally. But, we also must grow in wisdom, knowledge, and understanding of all things pertaining to the Kingdom of God. We must grow into spiritual maturity so that when it is our turn to instruct the younger generation, we will know how to do it right. It's time to grow.

Just Pray

Why should I pray for you? Why should you pray for me?

Let's see...What do you think would have happened in the book of John when the Pharisees brought the woman to Jesus? The woman that was "taken in the very act of adultery"...They brought her to Jesus, ready to have her stoned to death...BUT...What if they had all fallen on their knees and began praying for her instead??? What if they had known COMPASSION and INTERCESSORY PRAYER, instead of CONDEMNATION and "look at me, I'm praying" prayer??? Well, for her, I don't think the story could have ended any better as it is...BUT for them...well, I believe that they wouldn't have had to walk away from Him in shame, had they done things differently...

I read that Job was being "tried" by God...but he was being "attacked" by Satan...during this time, Job was covered with boils from the top of his head to the soles of his feet, he had scraped himself all over with a piece of pottery, his body was fevered, he became emaciated, he hurt so bad he wanted to die, and in fact, he wished he had never been born...we can probably agree that the enemy had him pinned down...his "friends" came to "comfort" him, but what they really did was point, accuse and condemn...they were NO comfort to him...

So, why should we pray for one another???

In Job 23:8-9, Job says, "Behold, I go forward, but he is not there; and backward, but I cannot perceive him: On the left hand, where he doth work, but I cannot behold him: he hideth himself on the right hand, that I cannot see him:"

The enemy had Job so burdened down, that Job couldn't "find" God!!! But it is obvious he was SEEKING Him!!!

Have you ever been under such an attack from the enemy that you couldn't even pray for yourself? Have you ever been so burdened down that you couldn't seem to find God anywhere? I HAVE!!! Have you felt the stones being thrown from your "friends" during the time that you sincerely needed them to be praying for you instead? Have you felt that you were all alone in the world with the enemy of your soul, who was trying his level best to destroy you? I HAVE!!! Or, maybe you were under such an attack, the enemy had you so blinded, that you didn't even realize what was happening, you didn't even know you were in need of prayer for what was going on...and if others could see it, OH MY, wouldn't you want them to be praying for you?!? I KNOW I WOULD!!!

Lord, help me to see what You would have me to see in another's situation. Help me to see them through eyes of COMPASSION and NOT CONDEMNATION. Help me to KNOW when to INTERCEDE for others. Enable me to pray the prayer that is needful for them. And last, Lord, grant it to me to be on the receiving end of the same, in Jesus' Name.

Justified by Faith

As human beings, or I should say, OUR FLESH, wants us to be okay, or right, or JUSTIFIED, in everything we say and do. BUT, we need to be careful, or we will actually FEEL that we are justified in everything we say and do. Why do we need to watch this? Because WE are not the ones who are qualified to make that call, GOD is. And if we did try, in our own minds, to justify ourselves, we would be way off base.

First, let me say that justification is defined as a declaration of innocence or righteousness. I could say to the Lord, "I am righteous", and wave my self-declared righteousness flag for the Lord to see, but what do you think He would be seeing?

Isaiah 64:6a says, "But we are all as an unclean thing, and ALL our righteousnesses are as filthy rags"...OH, I DO NOT WANT HIM TO FIND ME WAVING THAT FILTHY FLAG, PROCLAIMING MY OWN RIGHTEOUSNESS!! I and He would so much rather that I wave a WHITE FLAG OF SURRENDER!! Thereby confessing that I don't have it all together, and, in fact, do not have the ability to GET it all together without Him.

BUT, this isn't just about how we should think or feel, or even just about being justified. This is about FAITH. And just how good God is to us.

Romans 5:1 says, "Therefore being justified BY FAITH, we have peace with God through our Lord Jesus Christ:"...Well, that leads to another question. If faith is what justifies us, how do we get it? Let's see...

Romans 12:3b says, "according as God hath dealt to every man the measure of faith!" WHAT!?!

God gave us ALL a measure of faith!! He gave us a HEAD START!!

Romans 10:17 says, "So then faith cometh by hearing, and hearing by the word of God." OH, PRAISE THE LORD!! Now we know that, not only did He give us a head start of faith to begin with, but He also gave us the means to get more!! He WANTS to be able to declare us righteous!! He WANTS us to be justified!!

And not only that, this is the best part!! He didn't give us the head start faith, and then the means to get more faith just so we might be justified...ARE YOU READY??

Ephesians 6:16 says, "Above all, taking the shield of faith, wherewith ye shall be able to quench all the fiery darts of the wicked." OH, I'M ABOUT TO START SHOUTING!! the SHIELD OF FAITH!! OUR SHIELD IS MADE OF FAITH!! HE GAVE US WHAT!?!

He gave us a measure of FAITH...AND the means to get MORE!! TO BUILD OUR SHIELD!! AND OH, MY GOODNESS!! TO WHAT!?! Fend off?? Block?? Deflect?? NO!! TO QUENCH!! OUR SHIELD OF FAITH PUTS OUT THE FIRE IN THOSE DARTS!! To QUENCH means to EXTINGUISH!!

We need to understand that EVERY SINGLE ONE of the enemy's darts is a LIE!! Our shield will not only EXTINGUISH the fire in those darts, it will also EXPOSE them for the LIES that they are!! GOD WANTS US TO WIN!! AND HE HAS BEEN HELPING US ALL ALONG!!

PRAISE THE LORD!!

Know His Love

JESUS LOVES ME THIS I KNOW...FOR THE BIBLE TELLS ME SO...

I remember singing this song as a child. I remember teaching it to my children. It seems to be the first "church" song we teach to our little ones. Most all of us know it...BUT DO WE KNOW IT??

The first line of the song, makes a statement (Jesus loves me), then it tells why this statement is true (and I know this because the Bible tells me that it's so). I haven't found in the Bible where it says, "Jesus loves Katina" ...BUT...the ENTIRE BIBLE tells IN GREAT DETAIL...JUST HOW MUCH...HE DOES LOVE ME!!

Oh, that we could KNOW His love for us, and NOT just because the Bible says it!! That we could not only KNOW, but understand HOW MUCH He loves us!!

That we could ACCEPT HIS LOVE, LIVE IN IT, WALK IN IT, help others to know it and to KNOW it!!

I don't have a specific Scripture location to tell you of His love unless you read...Genesis 1:1 through Revelation 22:21...It is the story of His love for us. It is the greatest love story of all time!

Thank you, Lord for loving me. Thank you, Lord for enabling me to KNOW it. Thank you, Lord for allowing me to be a part of Your love story.

Learn It

I was raised in church, taught all the "Bible stories" as a child, taught that there is a certain way you have to live in order to make it to Heaven (right from wrong), or else you go to hell. I was taught that there is a God who takes care of us. I was taught that there was a man named Jesus that did not sin and was so good a man that He took it upon Himself to be beaten, ridiculed, and killed for all the wrong that I have done or may do in my life.

Well, I am thankful for all of this teaching. BUT I am most thankful that somewhere along the way, I learned (maybe by people, but certainly by the revelation of God, thank you, Lord) that, "ALL Scripture is given by inspiration of God, and is profitable for doctrine, for reproof, for correction, for instruction in righteousness:" 2 Timothy 3:16

Now, as I was pondering this, I began to think on another passage of Scripture.

Galatians 5:19-21 says, "Now the works of the flesh are manifest, which are these; Adultery, fornication, uncleanness, lasciviousness, Idolatry, witchcraft, hatred, variance, emulations, wrath, strife, seditions, heresies, Envyings, murders, drunkenness, revellings, and such like: of the which I tell you before, as I have also told you in time past, that they which do such things shall not inherit the kingdom of God."

I remember thinking (during a time when I was living contrary to what I had been taught), that I was doing okay because I wasn't out killing people. I guess in the midst of my deception and ignorance, this is how I measured that I was "okay" with the Lord. If you look back at how the works of the flesh are listed...#1 to envy someone comes before murder...OH MY! and #2 if I am not sure what all those other "big" words mean, wouldn't it be smart for me to look them up, because these are works of the flesh, and since I am flesh, that means I am NOT incapable of committing any of these things that would keep me from inheriting the kingdom of God!

Hosea 4:6a says, "My people are destroyed for lack of knowledge: because thou hast rejected knowledge, I will also reject thee,"

One last thing, it is possible to sin through ignorance according to Leviticus 4:2b which says, "If a soul shall sin through ignorance against any of the commandments of the Lord concerning things which ought not to be done, and shall do against any of them:"

Brother or sister in Christ, if you do not know the meaning of a word, look it up. What good is it to read a word if you don't know what it means? I hope this is a help and an encouragement to all who read it.

Let's Be Friends

I had a friend that I have known since childhood. We grew up together. We went to church together. I guess you would say we were best friends, for a time.

She had gone through a situation that had been very difficult for her. I knew this. We had talked about it more than once. I was aware of most of the details between her and the other person involved.

As a friend, I am supposed to listen, sympathize, and agree. Right? With whatever is being said, right? Not necessarily.

During one of our conversations, she was saying things that did not need to be said about the other person. Some of it was speculation. Some of it may have been true, but I didn't know it to be factual.

Basically, what I did was tell her that I didn't know it to be true because I had not witnessed it myself.

So, I assume that she took that as me defending the other person, and disagreeing with her.

Friends don't do that, right?

A friend is a person whom you like and trust. A friend is a person whom you regard with affection and loyalty.

Godly friendships motivate people to be godly.

"The choice of one's friends is a matter of wisdom versus folly."

Proverbs 27:17 says, "Iron sharpeneth iron; so a man sharpeneth the countenance of his friend."

When two pieces of iron are rubbed together, they shape and sharpen one another. They make one another more useful, efficient, better.

The same thing goes for true friends.

Proverbs 27:6 says, "Faithful are the wounds of a friend; but the kisses of an enemy are deceitful."

True friends will tell you the truth, even when it's not in agreement with what you are saying.

Even when it's not what you want to hear.

Lord, help me to use wisdom when choosing my friends. Help me to always be a true and godly friend, even if it costs me a friend. Help me to have true and godly friends who will tell me the truth even if it goes against what I want to hear at the time. Then, enable me to receive the truth with grace, which will allow me to change my perspective. I thank You, Lord, for this lesson, and I ask that You forgive me for each and every time I have fallen short in this area, in Jesus' Name.

Lord Willing

The Bible is full of true stories, historical accounts, and much more. It also has practical daily instructions for us.

Often, we think that we control everything. We do not. We make plans, but we don't even know if we will be able to carry out the plans we make.

I read a particular passage of Scripture, and the simplicity of it made such an impact on me that I catch myself saying it all the time...

James 4:13-17 says, "Go to now, ye that say, To day or to morrow we will go into such a city, and continue there a year, and buy and sell, and get gain: Whereas ye know not what shall be on the morrow. For what is your life? It is even a vapour, that appeareth for a little time, and then vanisheth away. For that ye ought to say, IF THE LORD WILL, we shall live, and do this, or that. But now ye rejoice in your boastings: all such rejoicing is evil. Therefore to him that knoweth to do good, and doeth it not, to him it is sin."

WOW!! Something so simple that we do ALL THE TIME is considered evil in the sight of the Lord...

You may ask me if I am going to work tomorrow, and I may say that I am.

But what I should say is, "Yes, IF THE LORD IS WILLING."

I may have PLANS to go to work tomorrow, BUT, I "know not what shall be on the morrow".

Lord, help me to ALWAYS consider this when I voice my plans. Although I may have made plans for tomorrow, I DO NOT know what tomorrow holds. I DO NOT want You, Lord, to look on me and see "evil rejoicing", "boasting" of my plans, in Jesus' Name.

Love God and One Another

The Ten Commandments

1- Thou shalt have no other gods before me.

2- Thou shalt not make unto thee any graven image,

3- Thou shalt not take the name of the Lord thy God in vain;

4- Remember the sabbath day, to keep it holy.

5- Honour thy father and thy mother.

6- Thou shalt not kill.

7- Thou shalt not commit adultery.

8- Thou shalt not steal.

9- Thou shalt not bear false witness against thy neighbor.

10- Thou shalt not covet, anything that is thy neighbor's.

First, shalt means should. Read them again saying "should". Second, shall means will. Read them again saying "will". If the ten commandments said shall instead of shalt, free will would not exist in these areas.

Now, who do you offend if you break any of these commandments?

1 through 4 would offend God. 5 would offend your parents. 6 through 10 would offend the ones that you commit them against.

These commandments are about how you love and reverence God, and how you treat other people.

Matthew 22:34-40 says, "But when the Pharisees had heard that he had put the Sadducees to silence, they were gathered together. Then one of them, which was a lawyer, asked him a question, tempting him, and saying, Master, which is the great commandment in the law? Jesus said unto him, Thou shalt love the Lord thy God with all thy heart, and with all thy soul, and with all thy mind. This is the first and great commandment. And the second is like unto it, Thou shalt love thy neighbour as thyself. On these two commandments hang all the law and the prophets."

Lord, help us to love You above all and everything. Enable us to love each other as we love ourselves, in Jesus' Name.

Measure 1

The Lord impressed upon me to study the word measure.

Leviticus 19:35-36 says, "Ye shall do no unrighteousness in judgment, in meteyard, in weight, or in measure. Just balances, just weights, a just ephah, and a just hin, shall ye have: I am the Lord your God which brought you out of the land of Egypt."

An ephah is a dry measure, one tenth of an homer, or one bushel.

A hin is a liquid measure, one gallon, or 3.7 liters.

A meteyard is a length measure, or a yard.

This passage of Scripture is referring to actual measurements the children of Israel used when buying, selling, and trading.

Deuteronomy 25:13-15 says, "Thou shalt not have in thy bag divers weights, a great and a small.

Thou shalt not have in thine house divers measures, a great and a small. But thou shalt have a perfect and just weight, a perfect and just measure shalt thou have: that thy days may be lengthened in the land which the Lord thy God giveth thee."

The children of Israel were forbidden (with consequences) to even POSSESS unjust weights and measures, let alone use them. Then they broke this law by "falsifying the balances".

Amos 8:4-7 says, "Hear this, O ye that swallow up the needy, even to make the poor of the land to fail, Saying, When will the moon be gone that we may sell corn? and the sabbath that we may set forth wheat, making the ephah small, and the shekel great, and falsifying the balances by deceit? That we may buy the poor for silver, and the needy for a pair of shoes; yea, and sell the refuse (chaff) of the wheat?

The Lord hath sworn by the excellency of Jacob, Surely I will never forget any of their works."

Even after this, they were still doing it.

Micah 6:10-11 says, "Are there yet (still) the treasures of wickedness in the house of the wicked, and the scant measure that is abominable? Shall I count them pure with the wicked balances and with the deceitful weights?"

Scant means insufficient or to supply sparingly.

Now, I want to show you something. Look at Leviticus 19:35-36 again. "Ye shall do no unrighteousness in judgment" and "in thy bag or in thine house". Whether they were at home or going out (with their bags), they were not to do any unrighteousness in judgment.

The word measure means to estimate or JUDGE the quality or value of something (or someone).

They were using SCANT measurements IN THEIR OWN HOUSES, insufficient and sparingly.

Do we also use scant measurements at home while we heap judgment on others? Is the judgment we judge ourselves with insufficient compared to how we judge others? Do we tend to judge ourselves and those of our own household a whole lot more sparingly than we judge others?

Can we measure or judge what, how much, or the quality of what is inside someone else? We can GUESS, but our guess, most likely, WILL NOT be accurate! We cannot see, judge, or accurately measure what is in the hearts of others.

So, the Lord commanded us not to!

Measure 2

Matthew 7:1-2 says, "Judge not, that ye be not judged. For with what judgment ye judge, ye shall be judged: and with what measure ye mete, it shall be measured to you again."

Mete means to use, to allot or to portion out.

To whatever length you go to judge someone else, it will be measured right back to you.

Whatever amount of judgment you pour onto someone else will be poured right back onto you.

Luke 6:36-38 says, "Be ye therefore merciful, as your Father also is merciful. Judge not, and ye shall not be judged: condemn not, and ye shall not be condemned: forgive, and ye shall be forgiven: Give, and it shall be given unto you; good measure, pressed down, and shaken together, and running over, shall men give into your bosom. For with the same measure that ye mete withal it shall be measured to you again."

Not only judgment, but blessings too!

Romans 12:3 says, "For I say, through the grace given unto me, to every man that is among you, not to think of himself more highly than he ought to think; but to think soberly according as God hath dealt to every man the measure of faith."

We set ourselves up as judges and evaluate other people, finding them guilty or lacking on some point. They don't measure up to our standards. When the Word indicates that we all have the same opportunity and have been given the same grace.

James 4:11-12 says, "Speak not evil one of another brethren. He that speaketh evil of his brother, and judgeth his brother, speaketh evil of the law, and judgeth the law: but if thou judge the law, thou art not a doer of the law, but a judge. There is one lawgiver, who is able to save and to destroy: who art thou that judgest another?"

James is saying that adopting a critical attitude toward fellow Christians is the same as slandering them. WHO DO WE THINK WE ARE?!?

2 Corinthians 10:12 says, "For we dare not make ourselves of the number, or compare ourselves with some that commend themselves: but they measuring themselves by themselves, and comparing themselves amongst themselves, are not wise."

We MUST measure ourselves by the Word of God! Not by one another! We are also NOT to use ourselves as the standard by which to judge one another!

1 Corinthians 4:3-5 says, "But with me it is a very small thing that I should be judged of you, or of man's judgment: yea, I judge not mine own self. For I know nothing by myself; yet am I not hereby justified: but he that judgeth me is the Lord. Therefore judge nothing before the time, until the Lord come, who both will bring to light the hidden things of darkness, and will make manifest the counsels of the hearts: and then shall every man have praise of God."

We DO NOT have the ability to judge the reasoning behind someone's words or actions because we can't see what is in their heart. We can't even adequately judge ourselves! Have you ever said...Why did I say that? or Why did I do that? or What am I doing here? - We can't even judge ourselves, yet we often judge each other!

The Lord also gave me an acronym for the word measure.

M-making

E-errant

A-assumptions,

S-severs

U-unity,

R-reducing

E-effectiveness!

We DO NOT need to be measuring, judging, or making assumptions toward one another! It is truly more dangerous than we think! To us as individuals and to the effectiveness of the Church as a whole!

Lord, I thank You for giving me this lesson. I ask that You help me to not only retain it, but to live by it as well. I ask You to enable me to reserve all judgment toward my fellow man. If a thought comes to my mind in judgment of another, I ask that You remind and enable me to take that thought captive unto the obedience of Christ, in Jesus' Name.

Messy Eating

My husband and I went to town. He asked me if I would like a bar-b-que sandwich for lunch, which is one of his favorite things to eat. At first, I didn't think about the WHITE top I was wearing.

My husband always likes extra sauce on his sandwich. I DO NOT, so when he told them to put "plenty" of sauce on his, I didn't say anything. Well, they put "plenty" of sauce on mine too.

I used about half a roll of paper towels trying to eat that sandwich, and by the time I was finished with it, I was not just a little irritated.

I DID NOT GET ANY ON MY SHIRT! PRAISE THE LORD!

As it took me about twice as long as my husband to eat, I was thinking to myself, "Lord, I know there has to be a lesson in this".

AND THERE IS!

I started studying what I could find in the Word about eating. Eating actual food AND eating the Word.

1 Corinthians 10:31 says, "Whether therefore ye eat, or drink, or whatsoever ye do, DO ALL to the glory of God."

Psalm 34:8a says, "O TASTE and see that the Lord is good:"

Proverbs 2:6 says, "For the Lord giveth wisdom: OUT OF HIS MOUTH cometh KNOWLEDGE and understanding."

Matthew 4:4 says, "But he answered and said, It is written, Man shall not live by bread alone, but by every word that proceedeth out of the mouth of God."

2 Peter 1:5 says, "And beside this, GIVING ALL DILIGENCE, add to your faith virtue, AND to virtue KNOWLEDGE;"

In these few Scriptures, we have gone from talking about natural food to talking about EATING the Word of God. The Word that comes out of the mouth of the Lord is KNOWLEDGE. He said we can't live by just natural food, but BY HIS WORDS, which are KNOWLEDGE.

Then He said we are to give ALL DILIGENCE to gain KNOWLEDGE.

Diligence means careful, steady, earnest, persistent, energetic effort.

So when we consume (eat, drink, or ingest) the Word of God, we are to do it carefully, steadily, earnestly, persistently, and with energetic effort.

This doesn't sound like "messy eating" to me. It doesn't sound like something done haphazardly.

It is done with care and purpose, kind of like the way I had to eat that bar-b-que sandwich.

And finally, Proverbs 13:4 says, "The soul of the sluggard desireth, and hath nothing: but the soul of the DILIGENT shall be made fat."

Natural food feeds our physical bodies. The Word of God feeds our souls. But we have to be DILIGENT when consuming it!

Lord, I thank You for using something as simple as a messy bar-b-que sandwich to teach me such a valuable lesson. Help and enable me always to remember, that when reading, studying, and consuming Your Word, I HAVE TO DO IT WITH DILIGENCE, in Jesus' Name.

My Defender

My family and I used to live in a house that we rented from a lady who lived out of town. When the opportunity arose for us to live somewhere else, rent-free, we moved.

About a week after the move, I got a call from my step dad. A local law enforcement officer had called to let him know that a complaint had been filed against me by my previous landlady, and the officer was coming by to talk to us; my step dad and myself. Now, I had known this officer since I was a child. We grew up together. I knew that he was a man of God, as was my step dad.

When the officer arrived, he informed me that the landlady's complaint was that I had stolen her refrigerator when I moved out of her rental unit. Let me go ahead and tell you that I DID NOT.

I told the officer and my step dad that I didn't do it. I let them both know that the refrigerator that I had had belonged to my grandmother, who had passed away.

My step dad, not wanting me to be in trouble with the law, said, "Well, just give that one to her."

My response to that was something like, "Um, NO, because it was my granny's, and she's not getting it!"

I understood the officer's position, not wanting to charge me, wanting to believe me, not wanting me to be in trouble. But with no proof or documentation, he kind of felt like his hands were tied.

It was my word against hers.

He even made the statement that he wished he worked in another county with people he didn't know.

But, this is how I felt to handle the situation.

Isaiah 54:17a says, "No weapon that is formed against thee shall prosper; and every tongue that shall rise against thee in judgment thou shalt condemn."

And...

Psalm 94:22a says, "But the Lord is my defence;"

I told them that the Lord had said in His Word that He would defend me. I did not do what I was being accused of doing. So, we were going to sit back and watch Him do what He said He would do.

I talked to the landlady a few days later on the telephone. I reminded her that I had my grandmother's refrigerator when I moved into her rental unit, so I hadn't needed hers. She had moved it out before I moved in!

She said that she had been mistaken. She had located her own refrigerator. She had also already called and cancelled her complaint with the authorities. PRAISE GOD!

The Lord just wants us to trust Him and to take Him at His Word. He can and will defend His children. And He can do it a whole lot better than we ourselves can.

Lord, I thank You for defending me. I ask that You help me to always put my trust in You, in Jesus' Name.

My Job

I work two jobs. One is full-time. One is part-time. Neither of my jobs pays me by the hour. I get paid a previously-agreed-upon amount for each task that I complete. So, when I get to work in the morning, I know what I have to do, and I know how much money I will be making that day.

How much I make per hour depends on how fast I work. That part is strictly up to me.

Our walk with Christ is no different.

2 Peter 1:3 says, "According as his divine power hath given unto us all things that pertain unto life and godliness, through the knowledge of him that hath called us to glory and virtue:"

He has already given us ALL THINGS THAT PERTAIN UNTO LIFE AND GODLINESS!

How? Through KNOWLEDGE.

Knowledge is familiarity, awareness, understanding of someone or something, which is acquired by experience or education by perceiving, discovering, or learning.

1 Timothy 4:13 says, "Till I come, give attendance to reading, to exhortation, to doctrine."

We gain knowledge by reading. By educating ourselves. By discovering and learning.

2 Timothy 2:15 says, "Study to shew thyself approved unto God, a workman that needeth not to be ashamed, rightly dividing the word of truth."

Just as with my jobs, if I work diligently and efficiently, I will be a workman that needeth not to be ashamed. If I read, study, and learn, I will not be a workman that needs to be ashamed. He has already given me the tools I need to increase my knowledge of Him. It is up to me how much time I spend doing that.

Lord, I thank You for all You have given me. I thank You for the ability and the mind that I have to read, study, learn, and know Your Word. I ask that You help me to increase in my knowledge of You even more. Help me to be diligent and efficient about the work I do for You, in Jesus' Name.

My Reward

God knows best, in that He does not allow me to know what all I will walk through before I actually have to walk through it, before I commit myself to walk with Him.

This sounds like He wants me to be "in the dark". It sounds like I will experience much suffering before I reach my reward. It sounds like I won't know it until it happens, the rough patches, I mean. BUT, He does it this way BECAUSE HE LOVES ME!

I now know, that being human, flesh as I am, if I had known what I would have to walk through before it all started, I probably would have run the other way. I can only say this because I have not yet received my reward. But if I had known of the afflictions beforehand, I'm sure,

WITHOUT HAVING RECEIVED MY REWARD, that I may have opted out of the race.

HOWEVER, I also KNOW, that ONCE I RECEIVE MY REWARD, each and every trial, each and every affliction, every heartache, every attack, every offense, will seem as though it had been nothing, ONCE I RECEIVE MY REWARD.

God DOES NOT want me to run the other way. He DOES NOT want me to opt out of the race.

He WANTS me to receive my reward. He WANTS me to succeed, to be VICTORIOUS, to OVERCOME. And HE KNOWS what I would have done, if I had known beforehand. I would not have even TRIED. I would have given up before I ever got started.

So, He doesn't let me know beforehand, because He NEVER wants me to give up. BECAUSE HE LOVES ME!

Philippians 3:13-14 says, "Brethren, I count not myself to have apprehended: but this one thing I do, forgetting those things which are behind, and reaching forth unto those things which are before, I PRESS TOWARD THE MARK FOR THE PRIZE of the high calling of God in Christ Jesus"

This tells me that I haven't yet made it. It tells me that if I stop now, all that has happened up until now, will have been for nothing. It tells me to forget about those things and reach ahead to new things. It also tells me to PRESS TOWARD THE MARK FOR THE PRIZE!! Do you know what that means?? I AM CLOSER TO WHERE I'M GOING THAN I'VE EVER BEEN BEFORE!! I'M CLOSER TO MY REWARD!! All of the tough times that I've already been through are behind me. I aim to RECEIVE my reward!

Lord, I thank You for Your wisdom. Thank You for encouraging me. Thank You for loving me the way only You do. I ask that You forgive me for my weakness and any fear of what lies ahead. I ask that You enable me to succeed, to be victorious, to overcome, and to keep pressing forward, so that I may obtain my reward. I also ask that if I can encourage anyone at all, allow me to encourage them to keep pressing, to NOT give up. Our reward, I know, will make everything else look like nothing. Lord, I thank You for Your mercy, which You give in abundance, completely undeserved, in Jesus' Name.

One Church

Ask me if I am a Christian and I will say yes. I will then, in turn, ask you the same question and chances are, you will say yes as well. We believe in God. We go to a church. We pray and read the Bible. We're not out breaking the law. We are Christians. Right?

While studying this after the Lord laid it on my heart, (thank you, Lord), I felt like I should be ashamed to raise my eyes above the ground in front of me.

Christian is defined as a person who has a personal faith relationship with Jesus Christ. It is derived from the Greek word *christianos* which means "belonging to Christ". Church is defined as Christians of all times and places, the interdependent ministering community of believers world-wide. If that didn't get your attention, interdependent means mutually dependent, or shared in common...YES!! ALL Christians world-wide are supposed to be INTERdependent!! On what?? On God AND on each other!!

The Word says in Acts 17:24, "God that made the world and all things therein, seeing that he is Lord of heaven and earth, dwelleth not in temples made with hands;"

Do we understand that when we assemble ourselves together and we say that we are "going to church", we are actually bringing the CHURCH to a building to assemble ourselves together??

Do we understand that the Lord is coming back after ONE CHURCH?? NOT A BUILDING!!

And certainly not any particular building in any particular city or town!! Brothers and sisters, we have to get it together!! By "it", I mean THE CHURCH!!

We think we have problems when there is division in our church building, our particular assembly of believers. But, OH MY GOODNESS!! The division in THE CHURCH that we choose to ignore!!

Paul wrote letters to the churches in Colossae, Laodicea, and Thessalonica. To the Colossians, he said this, "And when this epistle is read among you, cause that it be read also in the church of the Laodiceans; and that ye likewise read the epistle from Laodicea." To the Thessalonians, he said,

"I charge you by the Lord that this epistle be read unto ALL the holy brethren."

Oh, how much further would we all be in the Lord if we had heard every word He has ever uttered to a member of THE CHURCH!?! By our own acceptance of division in the Body of Christ, I am afraid we have missed quite a bit.

Our Battle 1

I heard a sister-in-Christ in church one time ask prayer for herself because she was "battling" something. Everyone could see that she was absolutely broken and DID NOT know any way to overcome or win that particular fight EXCEPT through prayer. She, I knew, was trying to live for the Lord, and had, in fact, already overcome SO many things, and she knew that to lose this battle meant sliding back for her. I am sure that she had prayed about it herself. But she had come to request help from the Lord through the prayers of others as well.

Afterward, this sister confided in me what this battle was. I immediately thought to myself,

"THAT IS UTTERLY RIDICULOUS! WHY IN THE WORLD WOULD SHE HAVE TO BATTLE SOMETHING LIKE THAT? THAT IS THE STUPIDEST THING I'VE EVER HEARD!"

AND OH MY-OH MY-OH MY!! DID THE LORD GET ME FOR THAT!?! YES, HE DID!!

I don't even know if I made it home after the church service ended before He got me! He said,

"Don't you see how broken she is? Don't you see how she's hurting? You may not battle what she does, but you DO battle. She only asked you to pray for her. But I am requiring that you pray WITH SINCERITY."

ASHAMED AIN'T THE WORD FOR WHAT I FELT!! He allowed me to feel her brokenness, her desperation, and not only that, but ALSO the brokenness that she would have felt if she had known my first thoughts about her battle. A helplessness in knowing that although she had asked for prayer, NO ONE was going to pray with sincerity. OH, MY LORD!!

James 5:16 says, "Confess your faults one to another, and pray one for another, that ye may be healed. The effectual fervent (intensely earnest or sincere) prayer of a righteous man availeth (accomplishes) much."

We can help one another to win each battle by praying with sincerity.

Lord, I know that I may not fight the same things that my brothers and sisters fight, so HELP ME LORD to NEVER look at them through judgmental eyes just because their battles are not the same as mine. HELP ME OH LORD to ALWAYS pray for them with a prayer that is TOP QUALITY, and NEVER one that I grabbed off the "clearance rack". HELP ME LORD to pray for them as if I am the one who is fighting their fight. HELP ME LORD to pray like it's MY ONLY WAY OUT, in Jesus' Name.

Our Battle 2

Continued...

Romans 12:1 says, "I beseech you therefore, brethren, by the mercies of God, that ye present your bodies a living sacrifice, holy, acceptable unto God, which is your reasonable service."

I have always heard this verse taught in a way that made me think a person had to be perfect to be used, or of any use to God.

It does say that we have to be holy, and acceptable unto God.

But, this experience with my sister-in-Christ shed a little bit of a different light on it.

Since the battle that she was facing was fast approaching, I was impressed upon by the Lord to offer to spend time with her during the course of her battle. You see, to have been by herself, I understood, would have made failure almost certainly unavoidable.

She needed support. She needed encouragement. She needed someone to stand beside her during her period of temptation.

So, the Lord showed this to me as offering myself a living sacrifice, to be those things for her.

Lord, help us to know when our brothers and sisters are facing a battle in which we could be a help to them simply by offering our presence. Remind us to be compassionate and to love them no matter what their battle is. Help us to present ourselves as living sacrifices, holy, and acceptable unto You, so that we may thwart the plans that the enemy has to take us out, in Jesus' Name.

Power and Authority

In Luke 9:1-11, Jesus called His twelve disciples together and gave them ALL POWER AND AUTHORITY...

This POWER AND AUTHORITY was NOT given to them as a "TALENT" to be hidden or buried or to be kept to themselves.

Then He sent them out to preach the Kingdom of God, and to heal the sick. And He told them to take NOTHING with them for their journey.

When they returned, telling Jesus all that they had done, He took them and CONTINUED to speak of the Kingdom of God, healing those that had need of healing.

HE LED THEM BY EXAMPLE!!

THEY AND WE have been given ALL POWER AND AUTHORITY! But this is NOT something we are to keep to ourselves! We are to go and tell others, heal others, share it with others! Furthermore, ALL that we need will be supplied. We are to keep doing or BEGIN doing what we have been called to do, using the TALENTS that have been entrusted to us, TO USE,

NOT TO HIDE OR BURY, even when it's difficult to do it.

Praise Him

Today, I just want to PRAISE Him! I THANK Him! I WORSHIP Him! I LOVE Him! I EXALT Him! I BOW BEFORE Him! I BLESS HIS NAME! I ADORE Him! ALL of this, I can do...AND SO CAN YOU!! AND IT IS ESSENTIAL!!

After thinking, praying, fighting, and struggling, I finally (THANK YOU, LORD) knew what the Lord was trying to tell me...

He had given me a word of encouragement for someone earlier, and it wasn't until 4 or 5 hours later that I realized what He wanted me to do...PRAISE HIM!!

I have thanked Him and praised Him for everything He has been pouring into and through me, BUT, if my thanks and praise were money, I believe He has allowed me to have the greatest discount ever known to mankind.

The word of encouragement He had given me earlier for someone else, I pray did encourage them, but no one knows what an ENCOURAGEMENT it was TO ME!! OH, MY GOODNESS!!

THANK YOU, LORD!!

The word of encouragement was about feeling as though you do not have a purpose in The Body.

Or better said, not knowing WHAT your purpose IS in The Body.

First, let me say this, Deuteronomy 10:22 says, "Thy fathers went down into Egypt with threescore and ten (70) persons; and now the Lord thy God hath made thee as the stars of heaven for multitude"... Don't you think with THAT many people in that congregation, at least SOME of them wondered WHAT their purpose was or IF they even had one? I'm sure they did. BUT THEY ALREADY KNEW SOMETHING THEY COULD DO THAT WAS ESSENTIAL!!

After the parting of the Red Sea, when the children of Israel had all gone over safely, Moses sang a song that started like this…Exodus 15:2- "The Lord is my strength and song, and he is become my salvation: he is my God, and I WILL PREPARE HIM A HABITATION; my father's God, and I WILL EXALT HIM"…Moses WAS NOT talking about a TENT!!

Psalm 22:3 says, "But thou art holy, O thou that INHABITEST THE PRAISES of Israel"…HIS HABITATION WAS PREPARED BY PRAISE!! OH MY!!

EVERYONE has something to do that is ESSENTIAL!! For the ENTIRE BODY!! I AM NOT saying that this is ALL you are there to do! BUT we ALL MUST realize that if we want to PREPARE HIM A HABITATION, if we want to be in HIS PRESENCE, and if we want Him to be IN OUR MIDST, WE MUST PRAISE HIM!!

Again, I just want to PRAISE HIM, THANK HIM, WORSHIP HIM, LOVE HIM, EXALT HIM, BOW BEFORE HIM, BLESS HIS NAME, ADORE HIM. I DESIRE TO BE IN HIS PRESENCE!! THANK YOU, LORD!!

Pray for Me Please

The Lord had laid it on my heart to pray for an individual; every aspect of his life. During the course of a conversation we were having, I told him, "If you get stressed about anything, just know that I am praying about it for you."

The response I got was, "I'm just glad that Jesus makes intercession for me." I have to confess that the enemy almost hit me with that dart! But, PRAISE GOD, I saw it coming and was able to avoid it, somewhat.

The enemy said that if he doesn't appreciate your prayer, then why waste your time? Why don't you just stop? He doesn't deserve your prayer! He doesn't even seem to want it!

Well again, PRAISE GOD!! The Lord immediately allowed me to see where I would not only be losing out for the person I was praying for, but for myself as well.

I just want to say that it would be absolutely amazing to know that someone has committed to pray over every aspect of my life every day. How awesome would that be!?! To know, if I get in a tight spot, that someone somewhere has already and is still praying about it, FOR ME!?! Now I know that Jesus is making intercession for me, for us all. And I also want to say that there aren't words to express how I feel about even one third of what He has already done for me.

There is WORD for us about praying for one another.

James 5:16 says, "Confess your faults one to another, and pray one for another, that ye may be healed. The effectual (producing) fervent (intensely earnest) prayer of a righteous man availeth (accomplishment of great worth) much."

We look at Peter and Paul, among others, as though we could never attain to their height in the Lord, BUT, they required, and even requested the prayers of others...Acts 12:5 and Colossians 4:2-3 and 1Thessalonians 1:2 just to name a few.

I, for one, desire, in fact require, and hope to inspire your prayer for me. Because I know that as long as I am alive, there is a deeper, closer, higher, unseen place to walk with God that I have not yet been.

Romans 11:33 says, "O the depth of the riches both of the wisdom and knowledge of God! how unsearchable are his judgments, and his ways past finding out!"

OH MY!! To spend the rest of my life trying to get as far as I possibly can will, I AM SURE, only be helped by the prayers of others! Thank you, in advance, for your prayers.

Preferring One Another

The Lord dealt with me in a very close area...my children. This is what I learned from my experience.

My two oldest boys came home from school on the bus. At the time, they were about six or seven years old. One of them said that a child on the bus had called his brother a bad word. I asked his brother, "Did you call him one back?" He said, "No ma'am." I said, "Good, you better not have."

I then explained to them both that the other child's parents may not have taught their child about Jesus and that that child may not know that you aren't supposed to do things like that. I told them that I was proud of them for not calling the other child something ugly. I also told them that I was sorry that they had been called a bad name but that people had been ugly to Jesus too. I told them both that they needed to pray for that child.

I am thankful for this teachable moment for my children. I am also thankful for this teachable moment for their mama. I really wanted to say, "What's their name, and who's their mama?" But, thank the Lord, by His grace, I did not.

Romans 12:10 says, "Be kindly affectioned one to another with brotherly love; in honor preferring one another;"

Philippians 2:3 says it like this: "Let nothing be done through strife or vainglory; but in lowliness of mind let each esteem other better than themselves."

I know some people might say that this is only referring to our brothers or sisters-in-Christ. I disagree. If the enemy weren't a part of this equation, we WOULD all be the brothers and sistersin-Christ that we are supposed to be.

We are supposed to, in honor, prefer one another. We are also supposed to each esteem others better than ourselves. This means to put others ahead of ourselves, our wants, our needs, OUR CHILDREN. To put others' children ahead of our own. OUCH!!

Proverbs 22:6 says, "Train up a child in the way he should go: and when he is old, he will not depart from it."

If we teach our children a lesson during an experience like mine, they will remember it and be better off in the long run. They will make better adults. It isn't always going to be easy. Ask me, I know.

Lord, I thank You for teaching me this lesson. I thank You for enabling me to teach this lesson to my children. I thank You for not allowing me to say what my flesh wanted to say. I ask that You always help me to use caution and wisdom during a teachable moment with my children, in Jesus' Name.

Ready Set Go

In 1 Chronicles 22, the Bible says that David "called for Solomon his son, and charged him to build a house for the Lord God of Israel."

In verses 14-16, David is instructing Solomon..."Now, behold, in my trouble (I have taken the time)...I have prepared for the house of the Lord a hundred thousand talents of gold, and a thousand thousand talents of silver; and of brass and iron without weight; for it is in abundance: timber also and stone have I prepared; and THOU MAYEST ADD THERETO. Moreover, there are workmen with thee in abundance, hewers and workers of stone and timber, and all manner of cunning men for every manner of work. Of the gold, the silver, and the brass, and the iron, there is no number. ARISE THEREFORE, AND BE DOING, and the Lord be with thee."

King David had made preparations by gathering materials, as well as men to do the work. The Lord had also given the land rest on every side so that the work could be done. So, King David told Solomon, you have all you need to get started, you have plenty of help, and you have plenty of time, ARISE THEREFORE, AND BE DOING!!

Although King David had gathered together and prepared an enormous amount of Solomon's required materials, and Solomon had enough to ARISE THEREFORE, AND BE DOING, or GET STARTED, King David understood that Solomon would still have to ADD THERETO, in order to be able to complete the temple.

THE SAME THING GOES FOR US!!

2 Peter 1:3 says, "According as his divine power HATH GIVEN UNTO US ALL THINGS THAT PERTAIN TO LIFE AND GODLINESS, through the knowledge of him that hath called us to glory and virtue:

HE HAS GIVEN US ALL WE NEED!! TO GET STARTED!! AND ACCESS TO THE REST!!

2 Peter 1:5-7 says, "And beside this, giving all diligence, ADD TO your faith virtue; and to virtue knowledge; And to knowledge temperance; and to temperance patience; and to patience godliness; And to godliness brotherly kindness; and to brotherly kindness charity."

It is up to us, to gather, or ADD TO what we have been given; the rest of the "materials" to complete our temple.

Verse 8 says, "For if these things be in you, and abound (are plentiful), they make you that ye shall neither be barren (useless) nor unfruitful in the knowledge of our Lord Jesus Christ."

Verse 10 tells us-"Wherefore the rather, brethren, give diligence (take care) to make your calling and election sure (secure): for if ye do these things, ye shall never fall:"

Lord, help us to ARISE THEREFORE, AND BE DOING, in Jesus' Name.

Right Spirit

I can remember throughout my life, in church, when I've heard a lesson or a message, or even just a word spoken that ABSOLUTELY cut me to the core. I KNEW it was right and that I, whether in my thoughts, words, or actions, WAS, OR HAD BEEN doing something VERY WRONG-something WRONG, according to the Word of God, I STILL KNEW IT!!

And what did I do? Well, one of 3 things: #1-let it go in one ear and out the other, or act like I didn't hear it at all, because I ALSO KNEW that to acknowledge that I had, in fact, heard it, I needed to change something, and ummm, NO, I just wasn't ready to ADMIT that, let alone actually DO it! #2-I would hear it, know it, AND acknowledge it, BUT, having "my arms around the enemy", I would allow it to just really BURN ME UP!, make me MAD!, and STILL not change anything, well, not for the better anyway! #3-I would hear it, know it, acknowledge it, AND RECEIVE IT...THIS would cause things to start changing for the better, FOR MY GOOD! THANK YOU, LORD! I KNOW THIS!! Yet STILL, sometimes I find myself trying to take #1 or #2...OH HELP ME LORD!!

In Psalm 51:10, David prayed, "Create in me a clean heart, O God; and renew a right spirit within me"...and what IS a "right spirit"? Let's see...

Isaiah 57:15 says it like this-"For thus saith the high and lofty One that inhabiteth eternity, whose name is Holy; I dwell in the high and holy place, with him also that is of a contrite and humble spirit, to revive the spirit of the humble, and to revive the heart of the contrite ones"... Did you get that?? He DWELLS WITH those that are of a contrite and humble spirit...AND He revives them!!

Contrite is defined as feeling or showing remorse or guilt... REPENTANT maybe?? Humble means having or showing AWARENESS of one's defects.

Not proud that I have had to learn this the hard way, being in this state, humble, contrite, and repentant, is the ONLY way I am able to choose #3.

Oh Lord, I pray that You create in me a clean heart and renew a right spirit within me. Help me not only to BECOME repentant and humble, but help me to REMAIN that way. Enable me to

ALWAYS hear, know, acknowledge, and CHOOSE to make changes for the better, according to Your Word, in Jesus' Name.

Seek Him

Over the years, I have heard the phrase, "seek Him" and now I have to confess that I never really knew what it meant. I also must confess that, when I had a problem, in the past, and someone would say, "I will help you pray about it", well, to me, that was like saying, "just deal with it".

NOW I know that, although I believed in the power of prayer, I wasn't doing a whole lot, if any, of it myself. So, maybe I based other's prayer life on what I knew of mine. Or, what I did know, was that I wanted an answer or a change in my situation RIGHT THEN. I DID NOT want to wait on ANYBODY to help me pray about it! Let alone, for God to answer. BUT THANK THE LORD FOR HIS MERCY THROUGHOUT THE COURSE OF MY IGNORANCE!!

I'm not saying I have it ALL figured out now. But NOW, I know what it means to "seek Him" and NOW I know JOY when someone says they will help me pray about my situation. Because I have learned that God's time to answer is the BEST and the RIGHT time for the RIGHT answer to come.

Seek means to try to find or look for. Well, I know that you just don't "look for" or "try to find" Him like you're hunting Easter eggs. With the attitude that if you find them, fine, and if you don't, no big deal. Or say, oh well, somebody else can find them.

The word seek is derived from the Greek word *zeteo* which means to give ATTENTION and PRIORITY to, to DESIRE, to CHOOSE TO FOLLOW. OH GOODNESS!! That sounds like a whole lot more than looking for something.

So, just HOW do we SEEK HIM?? Let's see...

Psalm 86:3-5 says, "Be merciful unto me, O Lord: for I CRY UNTO THEE DAILY. Rejoice the soul of thy servant: for UNTO THEE, O LORD, DO I LIFT UP MY SOUL. For thou, Lord, art good, and ready to forgive; and plenteous in mercy unto all them that CALL UPON THEE."

Psalm 27:14 says, "WAIT ON THE LORD: be of good courage, and he shall strengthen thine heart: wait, I say, on the Lord."

Psalm 70:4 says, "Let all those that seek thee rejoice and be glad in thee: and let such as love thy salvation SAY CONTINUALLY, LET GOD BE MAGNIFIED."

Psalm 119:2 says, "Blessed are they that keep his testimonies, and that seek him with the WHOLE HEART."

And finally, 2 Chronicles 7:14 says, "If my people, which are called by my name, shall HUMBLE THEMSELVES, and PRAY, and SEEK MY FACE, and TURN FROM THEIR WICKED WAYS; then will I hear from heaven, and will forgive their sin, and will heal their land."

Lord, I pray that You enable me to TURN FROM MY WICKED WAYS, HUMBLE MYSELF, and PRAY (SEEK YOUR FACE), CRYING UNTO YOU DAILY, LIFTING UP MY SOUL UNTO YOU WITH MY WHOLE HEART, CONTINUALLY PRAISING YOU, AND WAITING ON YOU, in Jesus' Name.

Seven Things

Proverbs 6:16-19 says, "These six things doth the Lord hate: yea, seven are an abomination unto him: A proud look, a lying tongue, and hands that shed innocent blood, An heart that deviseth wicked imaginations, feet that be swift in running to mischief, A false witness that speaketh lies, and he that soweth discord among brethren."

I have heard it said before that the Lord HATES these six things, but that seventh one is an abomination unto Him. An abomination IS something that causes disgust or hatred. So, the Lord hates ALL seven of these things. They are ALL an abomination unto Him.

Proverbs 30:29-31 says, "There be THREE things which go well, YEA, FOUR are comely in going. A lion which is strongest among beasts, and turneth not away for any; A greyhound; an he goat also; and a king, against whom there is no rising up."

As an example, this passage says there are three things, YEA, and then it lists four. You could read it like this: There are three things, ACTUALLY, there are four.

The same thing goes for the six things, ACTUALLY, there are seven.

1) The Lord hates a proud look. The EYES that look down on others.

2) The Lord hates a lying tongue. A TONGUE that tells lies.

3) The Lord hates HANDS that shed innocent blood.

4) The Lord hates a heart that deviseth wicked imaginations. A HEART that forms and entertains wicked or sinful thoughts.

5) The Lord hates feet that be swift in running to mischief. FEET that run from one evil thing to another. Where I'm from, we would say, "right outta one thing into another".

6) The Lord hates a false witness that speaketh lies. A PERSON who tells lies against or on another person. This is NOT the same thing as just telling a lie.

7) The Lord hates he that soweth discord among brethren. HE that causes disagreement between people.

All of these seven things are an abomination unto the Lord. BUT OH MY!

He hates the EYES that look proud. He hates the TONGUE that lies. He hates the HANDS that shed innocent blood. He hates the HEART that forms and entertains wicked or sinful thoughts.

He hates the FEET that are running from one evil or mischievous thing to another. BUT HE HATES a false WITNESS! THAT'S THE PERSON! NOT JUST THEIR TONGUE! And He hates HE that causes disagreement between people! THAT'S A PERSON TOO! OH, BE CAREFUL IN YOUR CONDUCT!

Lord, I ask that You continuously remind me to be cautious and diligent in the way I act toward and treat others. Help me to always be mindful of the way I conduct myself. I don't want You to hate me or any part of me, in Jesus' Name.

Some Are Missing

Have you ever just heard someone's name mentioned and "made a face"? If you have, be encouraged, you're not the only one. I've done it too.

A few years ago, the Lord had spoken to me about "missing Body parts". These are people who were once "in church" but since fell "out of church". These are people that we ONCE called brothers and sisters.

Well, at the time, I was sharing with one of my sisters-in-Christ, what the Lord had shared with me. While trying to explain it to her, I started naming names of brothers and sisters that were no longer "in church", and how important it was that we pray for them and try to win them back to the Lord. I said one name in particular, and this is what she said. "I have a problem with that."

And now I have to confess that, although it may not have come out of my mouth, I felt the same way about some people.

At the time, I could think of some that I would NOT want to sit beside me in church, whether they had been "in church" before or not. OH, MY MY MY!! LORD PLEASE FORGIVE ME AND CHANGE ME, THE ONE WITH THE PROBLEM!!

And this is not a new thing...Acts 9:10-17 says that the Lord sent a disciple named Ananias to lay hands on Saul so that he might receive his sight. Ananias, after all that he had heard about Saul, argued...verse 15 says, "But the Lord said unto him, Go thy way: for he is A CHOSEN VESSEL UNTO ME, to bear my name before the GENTILES, and kings, and the children of Israel"...OH WOW!!

Ain't we glad, as Gentiles, that Ananias obeyed the Lord anyway, even though he "had a problem with that"!!

Jeremiah 3:14a says, "Turn, O backsliding children, saith the Lord; for I am married unto you"...He didn't have a problem asking them to come back, He STILL loved them, STILL calling them children, STILL faithfully married to them.

In Matthew 18:12-13 Jesus said, "How think ye? if a man have a hundred sheep, and one of them be gone astray, doth he not leave the ninety and nine, and goeth into the mountains, and seeketh that which is gone astray? And if so be that he find it, verily I say unto you, he rejoiceth more of that sheep, than of the ninety and nine which went not astray"...

If HE is excited when one comes back, and not only that, HE goes out to seek them when they've gone astray, WHO DO WE THINK WE ARE??

1 John 3:15 says, "Whosoever hateth his brother is a murderer: and ye know that no murderer hath eternal life abiding in him."

1 John 4:20-21 says it like this..."If a man say, I love God, and hateth his brother, he is a liar: for he that loveth not his brother whom he hath seen, how can he love God whom he hath not seen?

And this commandment have we from him, That he who loveth God love his brother also."

OH LORD MY GOD, if there is ANYONE that I "have a problem" being able to love, ENABLE me! Oh Lord, ENABLE me to LOVE THEM like You do. And I thank you, Lord, for "putting me in my place", EVERYDAY, until I am EXACTLY the way You would have me to be, in Jesus' Name.

Something Better

When children don't obey or they keep doing the same "WRONG" or "BAD" things, they are called REBELLIOUS. Let me just say, there are consequences involving some sort of punishment for this kind of behavior. BUT the same word REBELLIOUS, can be used when you tell children, "If you don't clean your plate, you will not get dessert." The consequences then involve the loss of something children/we often think of as "better". A lot of the time, children will clean that plate in order to get that BETTER dessert. BUT, sometimes they will forfeit the dessert and refuse to eat the food on the plate.

The word rebellious means defiant; bold resistance to authority; disobedience; REFUSAL or FAILURE to obey.

The same concept goes for us as Christians, being in a state of rebellion AGAINST God isn't always just about, "You better stop doing that!" or "You need to start doing that differently!"

"A trusting attitude toward God and a faith that prompts us to respond positively to what He says will guard us against the rebellion that brought such suffering to Israel of old."

God, through Moses, led the children of Israel out of Egypt so that they might possess the PROMISED LAND.

Exodus 3:8a says, "And I am come down to deliver them out of the hand of the Egyptians, and to bring them up out of that land unto a good land and a large, unto a land FLOWING WITH MILK AND HONEY;"

The land where they were wasn't a bad land. In fact, when they originally went to dwell in Egypt, in Genesis 47:6a, Pharaoh told Joseph…"The land of Egypt is before thee; in the BEST of the land make thy father and brethren to dwell; in the land of Goshen let them dwell:"

BUT GOD WANTED TO GIVE THEM SOMETHING BETTER!!

Then when the children of Israel came to the promised land, they sent in spies to see the land; the spies came back and "discouraged" the people, the people were DOUBTFUL and AFRAID to TRUST that God had something BETTER for them. Because of this REBELLION, they were made to wander in the wilderness for forty years, and many of them died before they made it to the PROMISED LAND!

So, today, our land may very well have SOME milk and honey, and we may be satisfied with that. BUT God wants us to have something even BETTER! He wants our land to be FLOWING with milk and honey! He doesn't want us to SEND OURSELVES to wander in the wilderness and possibly never make it to the PROMISED LAND!

Standing

Several years ago, we had worked on a project at church, every day for about three weeks.

During that time, I developed what I assume was a heel spur in my right foot. For about 6 months I limped, and at times I could barely walk. Also, during that time, the Lord "dealt" with me to stand during worship service in church. Every service. Every song. It was as if my spirit would not allow me to sit. I would wince and move around, shift my weight, and even prop my right foot behind me on the pew as I stood. But I stood.

I didn't know the reason until what seemed like months later when the Lord spoke into my spirit these words..."If you will stand when you can, I will help you stand when you can't."

So recently, I had this brought back to me in a very real way. Have you ever wrestled and battled until you became so weak and weary that you didn't know what to do? KNOWING the Scriptures, KNOWING that we wrestle not against flesh and blood, KNOWING that you have the authority in Jesus' Name to rebuke the enemy, KNOWING that if you expect the enemy and recognize the enemy, you can resist and rebuke him??

Well, this was me. When I FINALLY realized what was going on, I felt like I had been looking for my glasses while they were on my face! I should have known! That's what I felt like.

Anyway, this particular attack (which was designed to take me out) lasted about a week. A very heavy battle. But when I told the Lord I simply didn't know what to do about it, He opened my eyes and not only allowed me to see it for what it was, HE HELPED ME TO STAND WHEN I COULDN'T!!

I rebuked that demonic spirit in Jesus' Name and IMMEDIATELY it was gone!! PRAISE THE LORD!! These words...GOD IS MY STRENGTH WHEN I AM WEAK!! WOW!! HE IS AMAZING!!

Straight Outta the Chute

"Straight outta the chute!"

That's what I said this morning when the enemy threw an ACCUSATORY dart at me almost before I was good and awake.

I went on to work, and all day he tried to plague my mind with it. But, the lyrics of a particular song would come to mind right behind that thought, EVERY TIME! I knew that even though the devil was trying so hard to beat me down, my God was trying to show me something, and WOW!!

The song goes like this...

We will overcome, By the blood of the Lamb, And by the word of our testimony...

I knew that this song came from the book of Revelation, so I looked it up...again WOW!!

Revelation 12:10-11 says, "And I heard a loud voice saying in heaven, Now is come salvation, and strength, and the kingdom of our God, and the power of his Christ: for THE ACCUSER OF OUR BRETHREN is cast down, which ACCUSED them before our God day and night. And they overcame him by the blood of the Lamb, and by the word of their testimony; and they loved not their lives unto the death."

Remember what kind of dart the enemy threw at me?? ACCUSING!! BUT GO GOD!!

I am made an overcomer how? By the blood of the Lamb! Not your blood, not my parents' blood, not a preacher's or a teacher's blood, and certainly not my own! But by the blood of Jesus Christ whose blood is the ONLY blood with the power to wash me clean and buy my redemption! Oh Lord, help me to NEVER think or act like or insinuate that MY blood has bought anyone's salvation! My blood HAS NOT accomplished one thing for anyone at all!

And how else am I made an overcomer? By the word of MY testimony! What does this mean?

Testimony simply means the evidence given by a witness.

So MY testimony is what I KNOW or what I have WITNESSED or EXPERIENCED of the

Lord. What He has done for me! The word of my testimony is my telling someone what I know of the Lord!

In Matthew 11, John the Baptist sent two of his disciples to ask if Jesus was "he that should come", and in verse 4 Jesus sent them back to, "Go and show John again those things which ye do hear and see:" He sent them back to give John the Baptist the word of their testimony!

In Matthew 28, Jesus told His disciples to "GO" and teach all nations what?? What they had learned from Jesus! They were to go and give the word of their testimony! HALLELUJAH!!

Jesus was setting them up to be overcomers "straight outta the chute"!!

Thank You, Jesus!!

Study It First

Deuteronomy 23:18 says, "Thou shalt not bring the hire of a whore, or the price of a dog, into the house of the Lord thy God for any vow: for even both these are abomination unto the Lord thy God."

You may laugh, and that is completely understandable. I did too.

I grew up in church. I've already said that. But, growing up in church does not mean that I read my Bible often as a child. I did attend Sunday School and Childrens' Church. I was taught the Bible stories that are commonly taught to children.

Somewhere along the line, I "learned" that it was a "sin" to buy or sell a "dog". I assume this idea possibly came from hearing this verse, or even from my grandmother saying that she would never pay money for a dog. It didn't matter that she never liked dogs anyway. I thought she was referring to the "sin" that I thought it was to buy a dog.

One day, at my mom's house, I was on the porch talking to some of the children. There are always children at my mom's house. Mine, and my nieces and nephews. They were talking about how expensive some breeds of dogs were.

I, with all of my superiority, told them that the Bible said you aren't supposed to buy dogs anyway. Go ahead and laugh. It was funny. Well, it was for a minute anyway. My step dad, who is a preacher, said, "That ain't what that's talking about." Keep in mind that I had children of my own, which means I was already grown. This is where a particular verse of Scripture comes to me...

2 Timothy 2:15 says, "Study to show thyself approved unto God, a workman that needeth not to be ashamed, rightly dividing the word of truth."

Believe me when I say I did study this topic. This is what I learned.

"Whore" in the Bible is referring to a female prostitute. While "dog" in this particular verse is referring to a male prostitute. The children of Israel had already been forbidden to become prostitutes in verse 17, which says, "There shall be no whore of the daughters of Israel, nor a sodomite of the sons of Israel."

So, in verse 18, they were commanded not to bring the "earnings" from these "occupations" into the house of God for their "vow", or their offerings. It was considered "dirty money". This is NOT the money earned from selling a dog.

During the course of this study, I learned a few things. It is not a sin to buy or sell a dog.

Prostitution is a sin, as well as the money earned from it being brought into the house of the Lord as an offering or a vow. I also learned that in order not to be ashamed when you try to "minister" to someone, you have to have already studied what you are talking about. You need to know what it means if you are going to try to "teach" it to someone else.

One last thing, there are many things in the Word of God that are forbidden. If you make money doing these things, wouldn't it be a bad idea to bring those earnings into the house of the Lord? If you steal something and sell it, wouldn't the money you got from it be considered dirty? Yes, it would.

Lord, I thank You for each and every lesson I have learned. I thank You that I have the desire and the ability to study Your Word. I ask that You continue to teach me. Enable me to be an avid learner of all things pertaining to You. Help me to be diligent about studying Your Word before I attempt to teach it to anyone else, in Jesus' Name.

Sword Practice

Would you agree that we are in a continual battle for our souls? Would you agree that we need a weapon to fight this battle?

Ephesians 6:17b says, ..."and the sword of the Spirit, which is the word of God:"

We need to KNOW the Word FOR OURSELVES and also that we might be successful fishers of men!

To know means to be aware of through observation, inquiry, or information; to be FAMILIAR with. We need to know the Word as well as we know our own families!

Exodus 23:13a says, "And in all things that I have said unto you be circumspect:"

Do you know what circumspect means? It means cautious and unwilling to take risks. Don't take for granted that you will learn enough by "watching" someone else use their sword. We need "hands-on" experience!

1 Timothy 4:13 says, "Till I come, give attendance to reading, to exhortation, to doctrine."

2 Timothy 2:15 says, "Study to show thyself approved unto God, a workman that needeth not to be ashamed, rightly dividing the word of truth."

If someone handed you an actual sword, would you know how or be able to defend yourself against an enemy who has had all of history to practice with it?

Our enemy in this battle knows how to use OUR weapon!! And he uses it AGAINST US!!

In Matthew 4:6, he even used it against Jesus!!

Not only do we need to be spending time "practicing" with our sword, we also need to be teaching our children and others how to defend themselves with it! How can we do that if we don't even know how to use it??

Lord, I thank You for what You have shown me of Your Word. I thank for the ability and desire

You have given me to study and know it. I ask that You help us to be willing to spend more and more time learning Your Word, which is our Sword, so that we may be able to defend ourselves against the enemy, in Jesus' Name.

Take It or Leave It

I was walking barefoot across the yard after it had rained. I am sure I have done this many times before. This time, I noticed that some of the sand was clinging to my feet with each step. But at the same time, with each step, some of the sand would fall back to the ground. Having never taken note of this before, I thought maybe I should see if the Lord was trying to show me something, and WOW!!

Isaiah 52:7 says, "How beautiful upon the mountains are the feet of him that bringeth good tidings (good news), that publisheth (proclaims) peace; that bringeth good tidings of good, that publisheth salvation; that saith unto Zion, Thy God reigneth!"

Romans 10:15 says, "And how shall they preach, except they be sent? as it is written, How beautiful are the feet of them that preach the gospel of peace, and bring glad tidings of good things!"

Matthew 10:1 says, "And when he had called unto him his twelve disciples, he gave them power against unclean spirits, to cast them out, and to heal all manner of sickness and all manner of disease."

verse 5a says, "These twelve Jesus sent forth,"

verses 7-8 say, "And as ye go, preach, saying, The kingdom of heaven is at hand. Heal the sick, cleanse the lepers, raise the dead, cast out devils: freely ye have received, freely give."

All of these passages of Scripture involve taking something "GOOD" wherever they went! The answers to prayers, perhaps.

Their feet were "beautiful" because of the "GOOD" things they brought!

But, verse 14 says, "And whosoever shall not receive you, nor hear your words, when ye depart out of that house or city, shake off the dust of your feet."

I learned by this that everywhere we go, we take something with us and leave it there. Are we taking good things? Also, everywhere we go, we take something away from there. Are we taking good things? Or do we need to shake off the dust of our feet? Lord forbid, that we need to shake off the dust of our feet before we go somewhere! MY OH MY!!

Lord, I thank You for showing me that I need to pay attention to my feet. Thank You for reminding me to pay attention to what I carry wherever I go. I ask that You always help me to only carry good things when I go somewhere, and to only leave that place with good things, in Jesus' Name.

Taking His Name

Exodus 20:7 says, "Thou shalt not take the name of the Lord thy God in vain: for the Lord will not hold him guiltless that taketh his name in vain."

I have heard, since I was a child, that "taking the Lord's name in vain" was the use of a certain two-word expletive. But, since the name of the Lord is Jesus, this really didn't make very much sense to me. I need to say here that I DO NOT speak that expletive. I also DO NOT like to hear it. I AM NOT saying that it's okay to say it.

When I began to study this, I noticed that it doesn't say "saying the Lord's name in vain" anyway.

It says "taking". So, I looked into the word take.

Take means to get hold of, to put on, to ASSUME, or to CLAIM.

Ephesians 6:13 says, "Wherefore TAKE unto you the whole armor of God, that ye may be able to withstand in the evil day, and having done all, to stand."

PUT ON or ASSUME the whole armor of God!

Ephesians 6:16 says, "Above all, TAKING the shield of faith, wherewith ye shall be able to quench all the fiery darts of the wicked."

GET HOLD OF or CLAIM the shield of faith!

Matthew 11:29 says, "TAKE my yoke upon you, and learn of me; for I am meek and lowly in heart: and ye shall find rest unto your souls."

GET HOLD OF, PUT ON, ASSUME, His yoke upon you!

So, when you TAKE the name of the Lord in vain, you are getting hold of His name for nothing.

You are putting on His name for nothing. You are assuming His name for nothing. You are CLAIMING His name for nothing.

You cannot USE the name of the Lord in vain. By this, I do not mean speaking it. I mean claiming to be His when you are not in a state of submission to Him. When you are not in a relationship with Him. I shalt (should) not take a man's name if I am not married to him. I would be taking his name in vain.

Again, 2 Chronicles 7: 14 says, "If my people, which are CALLED BY MY NAME, shall humble themselves, and pray, and seek my face, AND TURN FROM THEIR WICKED WAYS; then will I hear from heaven, and will forgive their sin, and will heal their land."

MY OH MY OH MY!! We have TAKEN His name. Have we taken it in vain since we must turn from our wicked ways? Help us Lord, in Jesus' Name.

The Front Lines

I am ALL FOR young people being saved and being filled with the Holy Ghost. I am also ALL FOR them living out their God-given purpose as they are led by the Spirit, wherever He may place them on the battlefield.

But, I have witnessed parents becoming jealous when someone else's "child" was "in the spotlight". I have also seen those same parents try to make a way for their own "child" to be placed in that "spotlight".

This is how the Lord showed this situation to me.

If there is a battle with two armies charging toward one another on the battlefield, where would you want your child to be placed on that battlefield? On the front lines? I think not.

2 Samuel 11:15-17 says, "And he wrote in the letter, saying, Set ye Uriah in the forefront of the hottest battle, and retire ye from him, that he may be smitten, and die. And it came to pass, when Joab observed the city, that he assigned Uriah unto a place where he knew that valiant men were.

And the men of the city went out, and fought with Joab: and there fell some of the people of the servants of David; and Uriah the Hittite died also."

David knew that to place Uriah on the front lines would get him killed. We need to be aware of this as well. This spiritual battle that we are in is no different.

I do not believe we need to hold our young ones back from their Spirit-led calling. But, we also should not try to push them to the front to get them in "the spotlight", knowing that the hottest part of the battle is on the front lines. THEY COULD GET KILLED...if it is us placing them there and not God.

Lord, thank You for our children. Thank You for calling and choosing them. Help us to encourage them where You have them. Keep them. Lead and guide them. Help us as parents to keep them covered in prayer and not to try to orchestrate their placement on the battlefield. But to place our trust in You, in Jesus' Name.

Tomorrow???

I must admit, I DO NOT LIKE FROGS.

Exodus 8: 2-4 says, "And if thou refuse to let them go, behold, I will smite all thy borders with frogs: And the river shall bring forth frogs ABUNDANTLY, which shall go up and come INTO THINE HOUSE, and INTO THY BEDCHAMBER, and UPON THY BED, and into the house of thy servants, and UPON THY PEOPLE, and INTO THINE OVENS, and INTO THY KNEADINGTROUGHS: And the frogs shall come up both ON THEE, and UPON THY PEOPLE, and UPON ALL THY SERVANTS."

This is already WAY too many frogs.

But Pharaoh, wanting to "prove" that he couldn't be outdone by God...

Verse 7 says, "And the magicians did so with their enchantments, and brought up frogs upon the land of Egypt."

Way to go! Now, ya got even more frogs! Wow! Nice!

And then...Pharaoh called Moses and Aaron to ask the Lord to take the frogs away.

So, Moses asked Pharaoh when he would like him to ask the Lord to remove the frogs.

Verse 10 says, "And he said, To morrow."...

WHAT?!?!? TOMORROW?!?!?

I know this sounds comical. But there is a lesson in it.

No, I do not want A frog in my house, let alone PILES of them.

The frogs were a PLAGUE! And Pharaoh was willing to spend another night with them in his HOUSE, in his OVEN, in his BEDROOM, in his BED, on THE PEOPLE!

2 Corinthians 6:2b says, "behold, NOW is the accepted time; behold, NOW is the day of salvation.)"

Psalm 46:1 says, "God is our refuge and strength, a very PRESENT help in trouble."

PRESENT means here. And PRESENT means now. Not tomorrow. Today.

The lesson in this is, don't wait until tomorrow. Get rid of the PLAGUE today, whatever it may be.

NOW is the time and NOW is the DAY of SALVATION!

Lord, help us to be willing to get rid of the "frogs" in our lives TODAY. Don't let us be willing to spend even one more night with them, in Jesus' Name. You are our refuge and strength. You are our present help, here and now. Thank You, Jesus.

Trees and Rain

One Sunday, before the morning church service, I went out to sit on the front porch with my coffee before my boys (I have 3) woke up. My nephew had stayed the night, and they had all slept in the living room. This is why I took my coffee to the porch.

My porch didn't have a cover or roof, so it was basically a deck. It was drizzling rain, so I was holding an umbrella over myself to keep from getting wet. I have to say that I have NEVER liked getting wet in the rain.

As I was sitting in the rain, having coffee, and holding an umbrella over my head, I asked the Lord what He would have me to study in His Word. This is what I got...TREES and RAIN...So, I began to search for anything I could find to study about trees and rain and...WOW!!!

I started writing down what I know about trees IN the rain. They don't have a cover to keep from getting wet. They get the full force of the rain, every time. They "stand" in the rain. They get sustenance. They are refreshed. They are renewed. They are cleansed. They are washed. They are strengthened.

Rain in the verb form means to pour out or pour upon; or TO GIVE IN LARGE QUANTITIES.

Rain in the noun form is defined as moisture falling from the sky, NECESSARY TO GROW crops and TO QUENCH THE THIRST OF animals and MAN.

"The ability of rain to cause the land to produce crops makes it an appropriate symbol of God's Word, which also "will accomplish what I desire and achieve the purpose for which I sent it.""

Psalm 72:6-7 says, "He shall come down LIKE RAIN upon the mown grass: as showers that water the earth. In his days shall the righteous flourish; and abundance of peace so long as the moon endureth."

OH, MY GOODNESS!!! LORD, POUR YOUR "RAIN" OUT ON ME!!! IN LARGE QUANTITIES!!! SUSTAIN ME! REFRESH ME! RENEW ME! CLEANSE ME! WASH ME! GIVE ME STRENGTH! QUENCH MY THIRST! CAUSE ME TO PRODUCE! HELP ME TO STAND!!! In Jesus' Name.

Urgency

When I was growing up and I would hear someone say something about "an urgency in the Spirit", I don't mind saying that it scared the daylights out of me. Well, today, I have been witness to something that is MUCH bigger than just an urgency in the Spirit, and WOW!!

Today alone, I have witnessed a CALL going out! OH MY! Not only to the ones who may not have YET had a personal relationship with the Lord, but also to the ones who HAVE!!

I know now that I have witnessed this before, but NOT like today. It hit me like a ton of bricks.

The heartbreaking look that must be on His face as He CALLS and PLEADS with people to just come to Him, and to come BACK to Him! OH, MY GOODNESS!

Matthew 22:14 says, "For many are called, but few are chosen."

I believe that today, the Lord let me know that not only is He calling to the "many" that are called, but He is also sending out a call to the CHOSEN! The ones that KNOW!! OH MY!!

YES!! YOU KNOW!!

And YES! WITH AN URGENCY IN THE SPIRIT!!

Lord, help me! Help them! Help us all! Open our ears to hear the CALL! Open our eyes to see Your will! Open our hearts and minds to KNOW the URGENCY, not only for ourselves, but for ALL! Fill us with a fresh outpouring of Your LOVE that will enable us to go out and lead others back to You! In Jesus' Name.

Value

Luke 21:1-4 says, "And he looked up, and saw the rich men casting their gifts into the treasury.

And he saw also a certain poor widow casting in thither two mites. And he said, Of a truth I say unto you, that this poor widow hath cast in more than they all: For all these have of their abundance cast in unto the offerings of God: but she of her penury hath cast in all the living that she had."

First, let's make sure we know what this means.

Penury means extreme poverty; destitution.

Living means an income sufficient to live on or the means of earning it.

Two mites were equal to a farthing. A farthing today would be worth one quarter of a penny.

Sometimes the Lord will drop a single word into my spirit. I will then study the word by the

Word to see what it is He wants me to know. The word for this study is value.

Value is the importance, worth, or usefulness of something (or someone).

We, as human beings, tend to look at others and try to assess the value or worth of whatever they may have to offer; what they have to "bring to the table". We do it to ourselves too.

The rich men in the passage of Scripture above may have done the same thing. They may have considered their offering to be a lot compared to the offering of the poor widow. But we don't look at things the way God does.

Is it better for me to just half-way give of myself because it may "look better" or "sound better"?

Or would we all benefit more if I give it all I've got?

What you have to bring to the table is just as important and essential as anyone else's gift or offering. We need to make sure we look at others' gifts and offerings with that in mind as well.

And give it all we've got!

Lord, I thank You for each and every blessing, provision, gift and talent You have entrusted to me. I thank you for everything You have given to everyone in the Body to benefit us all. I ask that You remind me not to try to assess the value of the gifts and offerings of others. I also ask that You help me to always know that no matter how insignificant my offering may seem to me, it is valuable and needed in the Body of Christ, in Jesus' Name.

Verify It

One time, I was teaching a weekly Bible study at church to anyone who wanted to attend. It wasn't a case of myself knowing more than anyone else, but of me studying and learning, and sharing what I was learning.

We had started in the book of Genesis and were trying to go through 2 chapters per week. We were all supposed to read those 2 chapters each week.

I would make a list of uncommon words from each chapter. Everyone would choose a word, and throughout the following week, they would look up the definition and any Scripture that mentioned their particular word.

I would also make a list of questions pertaining to the two chapters that we had read during the week.

Now, I have been guilty of looking at others, especially if they had been "in church" longer than myself, as though they automatically knew way more than I do. I found out during this Bible study that that idea is not completely accurate.

I had asked one of the questions and was waiting to see if anyone knew the answer before I showed them the answer in the Bible. When it seemed no one was going to answer, a sister-inChrist (who had been "in church" way longer than myself) told everyone the answer...THE WRONG ANSWER!!

I simply didn't know what to say, so I just showed them the correct answer.

I am NOT trying to make ANYONE think that I know everything, because I don't. BUT, I certainly do NOT want to TEACH or TELL anyone the WRONG thing. OH MY!

I understood a couple things at that time. Very important things. #1-If you have been in church for any period of time, you have surely been taught and preached to. But, have you read any of it for yourself? Or are you just assuming the answer to a particular question from what you've heard, without verifying it by reading it for yourself? And #2- Even if you have been taught and preached to on a particular topic, have you read it, have you verified it for yourself? Oh, please do before you begin telling others the wrong answer!

Wait on the Lord

Psalm 27:14 says, "Wait on the Lord: be of good courage, and he shall strengthen thine heart: wait, I say, on the Lord."

Isaiah 40:31 says, "But they that wait upon the Lord shall renew their strength; they shall mount up with wings as eagles; they shall run, and not be weary; and they shall walk, and not faint."

I want my heart to be strengthened. I want my strength renewed. I want to mount up with wings as eagles, run and not be weary, and walk and not faint.

How do I "wait" on the Lord?

Am I to just wait for a time or an event to take place? By sitting and literally just waiting?

Wringing my hands with worry? Twiddling my thumbs? NO!

A "waiter" is one whose job it is to serve...TO SERVE!

If you are a waiter, and you are taking the order of the Lord from the Apostle Paul's table; this is it...

1 Thessalonians 5:11-22 says...

11-"Wherefore comfort yourselves together, and edify one another, even as also ye do.

12-And we beseech you, brethren, to know them which labour among you, and are over you in the Lord, and admonish you;

13-And to esteem them very highly in love for their work's sake. And be at peace among yourselves.

14-Now we exhort you, brethren, warn them that are unruly, comfort the feebleminded, support the weak, be patient toward all men.

15-See that none render evil for evil unto any man; but ever follow that which is good, both among yourselves, and to all men.

16-Rejoice evermore.

17-Pray without ceasing.

18-In every thing give thanks: for this is the will of God in Christ Jesus concerning you.

19-Quench not the Spirit.

20-Despise not prophesyings.

21-Prove all things; hold fast that which is good.

22-Abstain from all appearance of evil."

We are to "wait" on the Lord by "waiting" on Him, SERVING Him. We wait on Him by doing the things He has instructed us to do in His Word.

Finally, Galatians 6:9 says, "And let us not be weary in well doing: for in due season we shall reap, if we faint not."

We Are Vessels

Genesis 2:7 says, "And the Lord God formed man of the dust of the ground, and breathed into his nostrils the breath of life; and man became a living soul."

Psalm 100:3 says, "Know ye that the Lord he is God: it is he that hath made us, and not we ourselves; we are his people, and the sheep of his pasture."

Psalm 51:5 says, "Behold, I was shapen in iniquity; and in sin did my mother conceive me."

We are vessels made by God, but since the "fall", we are born with the full potential to be filled with "bad" things. Some of these things are anger, bitterness, resentment, unforgiveness, turmoil, mercilessness, judgment, unrighteousness, doubt, fear, anxiety, criticism, pride, worry, envy, jealousy, weakness, foolishness, ignorance, brokenness, hate, and uncleanness.

Isaiah 64:8 says, "But now, O Lord, thou art our father; we are the clay, and thou our potter; and we all are the work of thy hand."

Jeremiah 18:1-6 says, "The word which came to Jeremiah from the Lord, saying, Arise, and go down to the potter's house, and there I will cause thee to hear my words. Then I went down to the potter's house, and behold, he wrought a work on the wheels. And the vessel that he made of clay was marred in the hand of the potter: so he made it again another vessel, as seemed good to the potter to make it. Then the word of the Lord came to me, saying, O house of Israel, cannot I do with you as this potter? saith the Lord. Behold, as the clay is in the potter's hand, so are ye in mine hand, O house of Israel."

When we become filled with the "bad" things (marred) over the course of our lives, the Lord (OUR POTTER) is willing to remake us. PRAISE HIM FOR THAT!!

Philippians 1:6 says, "Being confident of this very thing, that he which hath begun a good work in you will perform it until the day of Jesus Christ:"

Hebrews 11:6 says, "But without faith it is impossible to please him: for he that cometh to God must believe that he is, and that he is a rewarder of them that diligently seek him."

We MUST understand that He made us. BUT due to the fall of man we are born sinners, full of sin by the time we come to Him. That sin has to be removed and then replaced with "good" things. Some of these good things are faith, praise, compassion, humility, strength, joy, peace, love, wisdom, knowledge, holiness, righteousness, understanding, virtue, forgiveness, mercy, grace, wholeness, healing, gentleness, and meekness.

By FAITH we MUST allow Him to begin removing the bad things we are filled with and start filling us with good things.

2 Corinthians 4:7 says, "But we have this treasure in earthen vessels, that the excellency of the power may be of God, and not of us."

No longer will we be filled with the bad things that we and the enemy have placed in our vessels.

And we cannot remain empty because an empty vessel is useless. We can now be filled with the good things by the Lord.

2 Corinthians 8:12-15 says, "For if there be first a willing mind, it is accepted according to that a man hath, and not according to that he hath not. For I mean not that other men be eased, and ye burdened:

But by an equality, that now at this time their abundance may be a supply for your want: that there may be equality: As it is written, He that had gathered much had nothing over; and he that had gathered little had no lack."

This is speaking of giving natural things out of their abundance so that all would meet equality, and being willing to do so. The same concept applies to our vessels.

When we, as vessels, are filled with the good things, we MUST be willing to pour out to one another so that we all have what we need, and none lack.

Lord, thank You for making and remaking me. Thank You for filling my vessel so that I may pour out to others what You have so graciously given to me. I ask that You enable me to keep my vessel filled with the good things and to have a mind that is always willing to share with others out of my abundance. I also ask that if I am lacking in anything, You send someone to pour into me what I have need of, in Jesus' Name.

Well Done

My daddy passed away a little over a year ago. He was 74 years old. He had been a servant of Christ for all of my life. I'm 45 now.

After he had begun to forget things, he was diagnosed with Lewy Body Dementia. We watched him go through the stages of this merciless disease for about 5 years. For the last couple of months, he was confined to a hospital bed at home, where my step mother was his primary caregiver. He was also under Hospice care. I need to say now that I was not the only one who helped out, but for the purpose of this testimony, I will write of my experience.

One week before he passed away, I stopped by to check on them on my way to work, to see if I could help in any way. I would sometimes help feed him, trim his hair, clip his fingernails, and things of that nature. That day, he felt warm to the touch. I told my step mother he was warm and we checked his temperature. He did have a fever. We called the nurse. She basically told us that it was the beginning of the end.

I called in to work to let them know I wasn't coming in until further notice. I called and told my husband, who was at work at the time, that we would be staying at my daddy's house until further notice. During the following week, I only left about twice to hurry home to get clothes and such, just to rush right back. We would take turns sitting with Daddy, singing to him, praying for him and ourselves, and crying. The Lord truly moved in that house during that week.

Family and friends were wonderful. People brought prayer, fellowship, support, food, and other items. We are all forever grateful for the thoughtfulness and sacrifices of each and every one.

On the final day, I had gone into the kitchen to make myself something to eat. I got my plate ready and stepped back in to check on Daddy before I sat down to eat. From his breathing, I knew from previous experience that it wouldn't be long. I had been in the room when others had passed. I had seen some go peacefully and some not-so-peacefully. I put my plate away for later and went to sit with him. There were other people in the room with him, but I wanted to be there.

It was like I had to be there. I had prayed that his death would not be violent to witness.

My baby sister was sitting at his head on his right side, holding him and talking to him. I was sitting on his left side. The nurse had told us that the time would come when we would no longer be able to feel his pulse in his extremities. We didn't have a stethoscope. So, when the time came that I could not get his pulse in his wrist, I laid my head over his heart on his chest. His heart was beating strong for about a minute. Then it began to slow. I still had my head on his chest when his heart beat for the very last time. I looked at him and said, "You did good."

By this I simply meant that myself and others in the room had not had to witness a "violent" death when my daddy passed.

I am sure you may be wondering how I can even stand to write all of this. The peace of God is a wonderful thing! And the Lord gave me something else...

2 Corinthians 5:8 says, "We are confident, I say, and willing rather to be absent from the body, and to be present with the Lord."

Matthew 25:21 says, "His lord said unto him, Well done, thou good and faithful servant:...enter thou into the joy of thy lord."

I heard his last heartbeat. The very next step he took, was on a street that is made of pure gold.

The last heartbeat, and he broke the ribbon at the end of his race. I told him that he did good. But the Lord said, "Well done."

Lord, I thank You for my daddy. I thank You for the time we had with him. I thank You that he loved You and that he taught us too as well. I thank You for the peace that You have given me. I ask that You enable me to hear You say, "Well done" when I finish my race, in Jesus' Name.

Without Repentance

Romans 11:29 says, "For the gifts and calling of God are WITHOUT repentance."

I have heard this message before. It means just what it says. When God gives someone a gift or calls someone, that gift and calling are ALWAYS there. Just because the person may stop operating in the gift or calling, for whatever reason, the gift or the calling does not "go away".

God doesn't change His mind. That's the way I have always heard this message taught.

But, the Lord showed me this passage, or this message, in a different way.

Without also means outside of.

The first part of your life, before you "come to repentance", is BEFORE repentance, OUTSIDE of repentance.

Jeremiah 1:5 says, "BEFORE I formed thee in the belly I knew thee; and BEFORE thou camest forth out of the womb I sanctified thee, and I ordained thee a prophet unto the nations."

Galatians 1:15-16a says, "But when it pleased God, who separated me from my mother's womb, and CALLED me by his grace, To reveal his Son in me, that I might preach him among the heathen;"

Acts 9:15 says, "But the Lord said unto him, Go thy way: for he is a CHOSEN vessel unto me, to bear my name before the Gentiles, and kings, and the children of Israel:"

These are just a few examples of some who were CALLED, CHOSEN, and GIFTED BEFORE they came to repentance.

2 Peter 3:9 says, "The Lord is not slack concerning his promise, as some men count slackness; but is long-suffering to us-ward, not willing that any should perish, but that ALL SHOULD COME TO REPENTANCE."

Why is this so important? Of course, He isn't willing that any should perish, but...

There are those who have NOT YET COME TO REPENTANCE! That means that there are some WHO ARE CALLED, CHOSEN, AND GIFTED, who have NOT YET COME TO REPENTANCE!

And why is this so important to me? To us?

1 Peter 4:10 says, "As every man hath received the gift, even so minister the same one to another, as good stewards of the manifold grace of God."

1 Corinthians 12:4-7 says, "Now there are diversities of gifts, but the same Spirit. And there are differences of administrations, but the same Lord. And there are diversities of operations, but it is the same God which worketh all in all. But the manifestation of the Spirit is given to EVERY MAN to PROFIT WITHAL."

The word PROFIT means not only to benefit, but to BENEFIT OVER COST!

The word WITHAL means ALL THE SAME! A PROFIT FOR ALL!

The gifts that are given to every man are to BENEFIT ALL!

Hebrews 3:13 says, "But exhort one another daily, while it is called To day; lest any of you be hardened through the deceitfulness of sin."

The point is this...

Don't discount those who haven't yet come to repentance. There are those who are carrying gifts that will BENEFIT ALL OF US! We are to exhort (to beseech or beg) one another to come to repentance, to come to the Lord. Those gifts and callings are there. They are of God, and they do not go away!

Write It Down

The Lord had impressed upon me to write down things He had shown me. This is what He showed me through doing this.

If I start my walk with Christ at the lowest level of knowledge, there are basic principles that I do not know. I will have to learn a lot just to "make it".

But, if someone has written down their personal experiences during the course of their walk, and they are willing to share with me the things they have learned, there are some battles that I may be able to avoid.

Through our experiences, we are able to pass wisdom on to our children, and to others. With this information, they may be able to start their walk with Christ on "my ceiling" instead of "the floor", where I started.

Solomon didn't have to start "from scratch" to build the temple. King David had already done a lot of what needed to be done, gathering materials and the men to do the work. David had provided something that enabled Solomon to have a head start. Solomon was able to start on David's ceiling instead of the floor.

In Deuteronomy 11, God told the adults of Israel to teach their children ALL about Him. He instructed them to write it all down so that they could teach them for generations to come.

1 John 2:1a says, "My little children, these things write I unto you, that ye sin not."

I would love to know that my children, as well as others, could read of my experiences, things the Lord has impressed upon me to study, and revelations He has given me, that would enable them to avoid at least some of the snares of the enemy. So, they may be able to start on my ceiling instead of the floor. There are some things I would rather them not have to learn the hard way.

I encourage you today to write down the experiences you have in your walk with Christ.

Whether you stumbled and fell or shouted the victory, I am sure you learned something that could benefit someone else.

References

The Revell concise bible dictionary. (1991). Fleming H. Revell Company.

Hudson, C. D. (2006). *The KJV cross reference study bible.* Barbour Publishing.

9 781662 934780